THE FOOD LOVER'S GUIDE TO FLORENCE

THE FOOD LOVER'S
GUIDE TO
Florence

WITH CULINARY EXCURSIONS
IN *Tuscany*

2nd edition

EMILY WISE MILLER

TEN SPEED PRESS
Berkeley

Library of Congress Cataloging-in-Publication Data Miller, Emily Wise.
   The food lover's guide to Florence : with culinary excursions in Tuscany /
Emily Wise Miller.-2nd ed.
       p. cm.
   Summary: "Guide to the best gourmet restaurants and off-the-beaten-path locales
in Florence; now organized by neighborhood"-Provided by publisher.
Includes index.
   1. Restaurants-Italy-Florence-Guidebooks 2. Cookery, Italian. 3. Florence (Italy)-
Guidebooks. I. Title.
   TX910.I8M55 2007
   647.9545'51-dc22

                                        2006103044

ISBN-13: 978-1-58008-825-1

Printed in the United States of America

Cover and text design by Nancy Austin
Typesetting by Tasha Hall
Map designs by Fineline Maps, Oakland, California

10 9 8 7 6 5 4

Second Edition

CONTENTS

ACKNOWLEDGMENTS

Many thanks to Aaron Wehner, Melissa Moore, and Nancy Austin at Ten Speed Press, and to everyone who gave me their suggestions for places to eat and who came out to explore with me. This book is dedicated to Mark and Theo Rosen, both of whom are excellent eaters.

PREFACE

Perfectly preserved Florence, with its embarrassment of late-medieval and Renaissance riches, is one of the most visited places in the world. Like the prettiest girl in school, Florence's only problem may be overwhelming popularity. The city has never fallen off the short list of European destinations, and is a highlight on the itinerary of backpackers and mass bus tours alike. They come to see Michelangelo's *David*, the treasure-packed Uffizi, and the multicolored Duomo, and to experience the jolt of pleasure you get from crossing the Ponte Santa Trinità at any time of day or night and looking across the famed Ponte Vecchio.

The glory of this city crystallized over a period of three hundred years, roughly from the end of the thirteenth to the end of the sixteenth centuries. A lucky confluence of wealth from banking and textiles, a politically tolerant and artistically minded ruling family—the Medicis—and the ineffable and impossible-to-predict outcropping of genius embodied in the likes of Donatello, Brunelleschi, Leonardo da Vinci, and Michelangelo ensured Florence's place as the center and apogee of the Renaissance, represented in its architecture, painting, and sculpture.

In addition to the city's artistic splendors, visitors increasingly descend on Florence for its food. Tuscan cooking has become the best known of Italian regional cuisines, famous for its peppery extra virgin olive oil, hearty pastas and bean soups, and succulent *bistecca*. Here you'll find mobile stands hawking the workingman's lunch of a hot tripe sandwich, the famous *finocchiona salame*, and fresh Pecorino Toscano cheese. You can dart into an *enoteca* for a quick shot of Vino Nobile on your way home from the museum or grab a slice of rich *torta della nonna*, filled with custard and topped with almonds or pine nuts. And in the last twenty years, Tuscan wines have gone from watery slosh in bulbous bottles to award-winning boutique labels that fetch top dollar on the international market.

When I first moved to Florence from San Francisco, I thought I must be experiencing a kind of cosmic coincidence—I am a food writer; everywhere I go, people are talking about food. The house painter who sits down next to me at lunch wants to tell me the correct way to cook fish. I overhear the cell-phone conversation of a young woman on the bus: "Just a few slices of tomato and a dash of vinegar," she says, "we're going vegetarian tonight." At the beach in nearby Viareggio, the women under the *ombrellone* next to mine are comparing recipes for *ragù*. One argues strenuously for the inclusion of chopped prosciutto, while the other insists it's much more important to add chicken livers. "What," she says, "you don't put in any milk?" At this she shrugs her shoulders and makes a face as if to say, in that case the conversation is over and I can't help you, since you were obviously raised by wolves. Men walking down the street discuss last night's *bistecca*: "Was it too well done?" "Isn't it better at Mario's?" "Actually my wife makes it better than any restaurant."

Finally it became clear (as any local could have told me from the beginning): there was no cosmic coincidence; Florentines are simply obsessed with food. This is not a class-specific Dean & Deluca chichi kind of thing. Instead, it's an across-the-board cultural priority: Family, Friends, Food—not necessarily in that order (and wine is understood as included under Food). When I lived in San Francisco, I sometimes felt guilty that I was employed as a restaurant critic and was not doing "important work," like covering politics or writing scathing articles about the local electric company. As it turns out, in Italy, politics are pretty much a joke and food is dead serious. It is an integral part of life here, as it should be everywhere. We all need to eat, and in the long run what we eat, where we eat, and who we eat with affect the quality of our lives. Italians are acutely aware of this.

One of the most exciting things about living in Florence is absorbing the Italian way of thinking about food. You go to the open market and you buy what's in season and what looks good. Whether you're purchasing fresh porcini, Mediterranean sea bass, or radicchio from Treviso, if you ask the vendor how to prepare it, he or she will always rattle off a recipe on the spot. Not a "Well you might want to . . ." but rather "This is what you must do: no cream; you want olive oil, garlic, parsley . . ." At which point, the other buyers around you will pipe in with either agreement or disagreement, and at that moment, you feel particularly lucky to be living in Florence. And the recipes are always good.

I have a friend who moved to Los Angeles and always complains about the lack of good fresh produce and meats there. I like to torment her with tales of my food shopping in Florence. When I buy my fresh ricotta, the vendor asks if I want cow's or sheep's milk; when I buy veal, I can choose between milk-fed or grass-fed. Prosciutto? How aged? Sweet or Tuscan style? Fresh sardines? Not only can I buy them, but I can have them cleaned and filleted for the same price.

■ ■ ■

Like any food fetishist who moves to Italy, I arrived with a slew of books and several folders of clipped articles. I had excellent guidebooks covering eating in Italy, in northern Italy, and even in Tuscany, but nothing that gave more than a dozen or so pages to Florence itself. Someone once said that a friend gave him these directions to the best restaurant in Florence: "Drive into the city. Park your car. The first restaurant you see, go eat

there." This is a great story, and in many ways it's true. The average Florentine trattoria is usually quite good. On the other hand, if you stumble blindly into a trattoria just off the Ponte Vecchio, you might end up in a place that is touristy, overpriced, and producing lazy, mediocre food, because the proprietor knows he can get away with it. I wanted to write a book that would lead travelers to the best restaurants: the ones that use only fresh ingredients, that cook both traditional and innovative dishes, that are in the Center and off the beaten path. I also wanted to go much deeper into the Florentine food scene as a whole, looking at where the locals go for pizza and beer on a Friday night; where to get a quick lunch between sights without being caught in a tourist trap; and who sells the best selection of Tuscan and other Italian wines.

In order to find the best places to eat, I talked to many Florentines and other longtime residents of the city—cooking teachers, bar owners, and ordinary *golosi* (food lovers)—who gave me incredibly valuable advice. I also consulted other guidebooks, both old and new in English and Italian, and I scoured the city, keeping an eye out for new restaurants and *pasticcerie*, good-looking *enoteche*, irresistible *gelaterias*, and wisely stocked markets and other shops. I made an effort to search out places off the radar, some so far out that only dedicated food fiends will bother to track them down. I also tried to find that ever-elusive thing that Florentines love to talk about, the *buon rapporto prezzo/qualità* (a just relationship between price and quality). It is not important that something is inexpensive, but rather that you get what you pay for, whether it is a Sangiovese wine or a three-course meal. When I visited the restaurants, I went incognito (though not in wig and funny glasses), without announcing myself to the owners beforehand, and without being served gratis.

No doubt, some people will look at this book and find to their dismay that their favorite restaurant was not included, an unavoidable hazard of the trade. It may be that I never ate there, or it may be that I ate there several times and decided not to include it for any number of reasons. In any case, I've tried to include a broad variety of places in every price range. I hope this volume will be helpful and insightful for both travelers and residents, leading to many excellent meals.

■ ■ ■

A note on the second edition: When the time came to revisit the places in this book, I was a little afraid of what I might find. In the three years since the first edition came out, Florence has changed, Italy has changed. I was wary that everything would be much more expensive and touristy. Instead, I was happily surprised. Despite some problems (poor service, jaded owners, tourist traps), the quality of the food and wine in Florence and Tuscany is still amazingly high. This is because the people take pride in what they do and, in most cases, are *not* just out to make a buck any way they can. Family tradition and attachment to the land and the food run too deep for Florentines to abandon their high standards—at least not yet.

Buon appetito.

A local paper announces, "Salumi vendor condemned for selling a different prosciutto than the one requested."

INTRODUCTION

RESTAURANT BASICS

Ristorante, trattoria, enoteca . . . trying to unscramble the code words for "place to eat" will only make you hungrier. Luckily, the semantics of eating in Florence matters less and less. In the past, the hierarchy of differentiation among *ristorante, trattoria, osteria,* and the like was more meaningful, but the lines have blurred. A brief rundown of the remaining distinctions follows.

Ristorante: The term *ristorante* generally implies a serious place to eat, with linen tablecloths, stem wineglasses, and the usual fripperies of fine dining. It also typically means a more expensive meal.

Osteria: *Osteria* is a tricky one. It used to indicate a place to both drink wine and eat a casual meal, much like an enoteca, but is now usually interchangeable with trattoria.

Trattoria: A *trattoria* is traditionally a casual place to drink wine and eat home-style regional cooking—the kind of place with bare wooden tables and a flask of Chianti on each one. This is often still the case, but the word has also been co-opted by restaurateurs who want to charge fifteen euros for a plate of pasta. Or sometimes a trattoria has simply evolved over the years into a more formal, expensive destintation but has retained its original name. Trattoria kitchens usually churn out hearty, satisfying soups and pastas for primi and roasted or grilled meats for secondi.

Enoteca: The term *enoteca* is used in three diverse ways around town: it can be a wine store, a wine bar, or a restaurant that prides itself on its special wine list.

Mescita, fiaschetteria: *Mescita* and *fiaschetteria* once both meant "place to buy and drink wine," or a similar combination, but are now occasionally used in the same way as trattoria.

Tavola calda: A *tavola calda* is often just what it sounds like: a "hot table"—a place where cauldrons of pasta, soup, or rice are already stewing and you're served a quick, cheap, hot meal.

Reservations

Reservations are big in Florence. It struck me as bizarre the first time I walked into a casual trattoria on a Tuesday night and was asked, "Have you reserved?" The answer was no, and I got a table anyway, but I learned a lesson: it's always better to call ahead. In high season, this city is so engorged with tourists that restaurants have become reservation savvy. When you call to reserve, you'll find that many restaurateurs speak at least some English.

Prime-Time Dining

You've just arrived in Florence and you already know about a hot restaurant in town, so you call and make a reservation for 8 PM, prime time in most cities. When you get there, you find the place quiet and empty until you're eating dessert, when suddenly the crowd rushes in. Barcelona it's not, but people like to eat late in Florence. In fact, dining times are surprisingly circumscribed, basically 9 to 10:30 PM. Before that you might be lonely, and after that you can have trouble finding a meal. For lunch, timing is more standard; most people eat between 12:30 and 2:30 PM, with a concentrated rush between 1 and 2 PM. But fortunately you can always find a good snack or *panino* later in the afternoon.

Days Off and Holidays

Most restaurants close either on Sunday or Monday; I have indicated closing days as accurately as possible. And if you ever go to an Italian city in August, you'll witness a strange phenomenon: the tourists have the place to themselves, as almost all the locals head to a beach somewhere, anywhere, for their August vacation. In Italy, the August beach vacation is a right (and a rite), not a privilege. Italians would no sooner give it up than start eating ham out of a can.

In August, you're lucky if you get your mail delivered, let alone find open markets and shops. That's why it's better, if possible, to plan a trip to Italy for any other time of year, when restaurants will be open and the Uffizi guards are on duty, instead of lying on the beach in Elba. The city government is aware of the August desertion problem and has tried to organize things so that not every single service in a given neighborhood goes on vacation at the same time. August 15 is Ferragosto, a national Italian holiday, so expect pretty much everything to be closed on that day. Circling out from there, many shops close for either one or two weeks around the fifteenth; others literally take the whole month, from the first to the thirty-first; and still others have taken to extending their time away to include the end of July and beginning of September.

Many businesses also close for a week or two weeks around Christmas (until January 6, the Epiphany).

The Menu

With few variations, Florentine menus follow a standard order: *antipasto* (appetizer), *primo* (first course), *secondo* (second course), *contorno* (side dish), *insalata* (salad), *dolce* (dessert), *caffè*, and *digestivo* (after-dinner drink), all accompanied by *acqua* (bottled water), which comes either *frizzante/gassata* (sparkling) or *naturale* (still). Of course, there's *vino*, too, whether it's *della casa* (house wine) or from the wine list (see chapter 2 for more information on ordering wine).

Enough foreigners tromp through Florence that it no longer seems bizarre when a customer orders a salad first or coffee at the same time as dessert—just as it's no longer a huge faux pas to drink a cappuccino after noon. At some trattorias, you might still feel pressure to order several courses, but that's on the decline. I've noticed both Italians and foreigners getting creative with the menu by sharing a primo and each ordering a secondo; taking a salad as a secondo; or mixing and matching any of the above. Don't feel compelled to eat more than you want to. Just be aware that sharing a pasta and drinking only water is not going to make you popular with your waiter.

ANTIPASTI

A few traditional antipasti appear on nearly every menu in town: *crostini toscani* (toasted bread slices topped with chopped liver pâté) and *antipasto toscano*, usually a mix of prosciutto and salami plus the crostini. The latter will also sometimes include *fettunta*, slices of grilled Tuscan bread topped with olive oil and garlic. *Crostini misti* is usually an assortment of four toasts, topped with liver pâté, chopped tomato, artichoke spread, and sometimes mushrooms. The excellent local prosciutto is available year-round but comes draped over melon only in summer when the fruit is in season.

PRIMI

Though it is now synonymous with Italian cooking, pasta is not the preeminent first course in Tuscany. Before the twentieth century, on farms and in towns, Tuscans mostly lived on soups made of simple ingredients like beans, grains, bread, and cabbage. This *cucina povera*, or peasant cooking, is the backbone of Tuscan cuisine.

The quintessential Florentine primo is *ribollita*, a thick soup made from beans, bread, and *cavolo nero* (dinosaur or *lacinato* kale), though the bread and tomato soup called *pappa al pomodoro* and soups made from *ceci* (chickpeas) and *farro* (an ancient variety of wheat) are also common—and delicious. In summer, *ribollita* is often replaced with *panzanella*, a salad of bread, cucumbers, peppers, and tomatoes, all tossed with local olive oil and red wine vinegar. In addition to these standards, you'll usually find a good selection of pastas—typically sauced with artichokes, tomatoes, meat sauce (called *sugo* or *ragù*), or porcini, depending on the season—and a gnocchi dish or two. Polenta and risotto, both more common in the north, make infrequent appearances on Florentine menus.

Useful Phrases

Vorrei prenotare per stasera. = I'd like to make a reservation for tonight.

Devo cancellare la prenotazione. = I have to cancel the reservation.

Siamo in due/tre/quattro. = We are a party of two/three/four.

Si può sedere fuori? = Can we sit outside?

Vorrei un bicchiere di acqua. = I would like a glass of water.

Vorremmo ordinare una bottiglia di vino. = We'd like to order a bottle of wine.

Vorremmo condividere un antipasto. = We'd like to share an antipasto.

Ci porta la lista dei vini, per piacere? = Will you bring us the wine list, please?

Ci porta il conto, per favore? = Will you bring us the check, please?

Ci farebbe due caffè, per favore? = Would you make us two coffees, please?

Ci porta un menu, per favore? = Could you bring us a menu, please?

Vorrei un etto di pancetta. = I'd like an *etto* (100 grams, about $1/4$ pound) of pancetta.

Vorrei un mezzo kilo di cipolle rosse. = I'd like a half kilo (about a pound) of red onions.

A posto così. = That's enough.

Scusi, dov'è questo ristorante? = Excuse me, where is this restaurant?

È qui vicino? = Is it nearby?

Come si arriva in questo posto? = How do I get to this place?

Sono allergico/a, non posso mangiare X. = I am allergic, I can't eat X.

C'è carne dentro? = Does it have meat in it?

È buonissima, questa zuppa! = This soup is delicious!

SECONDI

Tuscan cooking, with its emphasis on soups, pastas, and olive oil, has gained a reputation as a light and healthful way to eat. But Tuscans love heavy meat dishes as much, if not more, than Italians from any other region. (Many people forget that although it's hot and humid in Florence in the summer and for most of the high-tourist season, it can get very cold in winter—down to the twenties and thirties—which helps explain the popularity of meats and stews, as well as all those puffy jackets.) The high-quality meats here tend to be cooked simply, often grilled or roasted, and can sometimes be too heavily salted for some tastes.

The secondo sine qua non is the *bistecca alla fiorentina* (see page 18), a thick slab of T-bone steak that is grilled until barely rare and served with only salt and olive oil as condiments. If you don't have the monstrous appetite necessary to dispatch an entire bistecca, another good choice is a *tagliata,* which is part of a bistecca that has been sliced and is often served with arugula and balsamic vinegar or shaved parmesan cheese. Other secondi to try include *arista* (pork loin roast) and *vitello arrosto* (roast veal), often thinly sliced and served with a bit of their cooking juice. Grilled chops are also a local specialty, especially the succulent *lombatina di vitella.* If you keep an eye out, you'll find such dishes as duck à l'orange (*anatra con salsa di arancia*), which Tuscans claim Marie de' Medici took with her from Florence to the French court; *coniglio* (rabbit), cooked in white wine, roasted, or fried; and other poultry and game, like *cinghiale* (wild boar) and *lepre* (hare). Fish isn't as common on Florentine menus, but some restaurants make a point of featuring it, in which case they might offer a *baccalà alla livornese* (salt cod cooked in tomato sauce), or sometimes a simple grilled gilt-head bream (*orata*) or sea bass (*branzino* or *spigola*). Only the new wave of chic restaurants offers true vegetarian secondi, but many vegetarians will be more than satisfied with a combination of primi, contorni, and salad—no one needs to worry about going hungry here.

CONTORNI

Most of us are used to main dishes that come with meat and a side vegetable or two on the plate. In Italy, you need to order the sides separately; hence, the *contorno* (side dish), brought at the same time as the secondo. Contorni tend to be no-nonsense to the point of neglect, but they do go well with Tuscan meats. The most common are *patate arrosto* (roasted potatoes); *fagioli* (beans), usually white beans cooked with garlic and sage; *spinaci* (spinach) or another leafy green that typically comes *saltati* (sautéed, usually with plenty of salt, garlic, and oil); and sometimes a summery *peperonata* (sautéed peppers).

INSALATE AND INSALATONE

Small and simple house salads are interchangeable with a vegetable *contorno*. The most common insalata is *mista*, a small bowl of lettuce, tomato, red radicchio, and some shredded carrot. Many trattorias also serve salads of plain arugula or radicchio, sometimes mixed with shaved Parmesan, along with olive oil and vinegar.

You can tell how sensitive a restaurant is to its tourist clientele by whether it features a list of decidedly nontraditional *insalatone* on the menu. These "big salads" of shrimp, avocado, celery, grapes, cheeses— you name it—cater to American dietary tastes but have also become popular with some Italians. They can take the place of either a primo or secondo and often have names like Californiana or Mediterranea. (I was saved by these creations when my mother-in-law came to town and announced that she was no longer eating carbohydrates.) Two good places to try an *insalatone* are Enoteca Baldovino (see page 82) and Coquinarius (see page 46).

FORMAGGI

If your menu has a cheese section, the choice will likely include one or two Pecorini Toscani (see page 24), Gorgonzola (soft blue cheese), or caprino (goat cheese). The cheeses often come drizzled with honey or accompanied by a confiture or tart fruit *mostarda* (a kind of chutney). You might also run across a nice stinky aged Taleggio from the north of Italy, or one of the mild and creamy mozzarella or caciocavallo cheeses from the south.

DOLCI

Many Florentines have a sweet tooth—apparent in the bustling *pasticcerie* in town and the many spoonfuls of sugar locals can squeeze into a thimbleful of coffee—but they are not as enthusiastic about restaurant desserts. A lot of diners opt for just *biscottini* and *vin santo*, or a simple plate of pineapple. Keep an eye out for *torta della nonna*, a local custard pie topped with pine nuts or almonds, or the occasional *zuccotto*, a concoction of sponge cake and sweet ricotta. *Castagnaccio*, a thin cake made of chestnut flour, sometimes puts in an appearance on local menus around Christmastime, but it is an acquired taste.

The dessert list at most trattorias consists of Italian standards: crème caramel, *panna cotta* (literally "cooked cream," usually a light, flavored custard topped with chocolate, caramel, or berries), tiramisù, and *torta al cioccolato* (typically a low, dense chocolate cake). If you're at a casual trattoria or pizzeria, ask if the desserts are *fatti in casa* (made in-house); you can assume they are at a more high-end place, which makes the prospect of a delicious slice of *torta al cioccolato* or fresh *panna cotta* that much more secure.

CAFFÈ

It took me a while to figure out that coffee is ordered *after* the dessert and not during, but I have come to anticipate the small, strong shot of *caffè* at the end of a long (or short) meal. When taken in small doses, it seems to help digestion without keeping you awake, plus it's a good way to counteract some of the wine you've just consumed. (For a primer on coffee vocabulary, see page 11–12.)

DIGESTIVI

Just when you thought your marathon meal was coming to an end and the bill was in sight, the waiter arrives to offer you a *digestivo*. Italians often refer to this as the *ammazzacaffè*—the "coffee killer" (funny because once the coffee has cleared your head of all the wine, you start the cycle all over again). Clear but deadly grappa served in elegant little cylindrical glasses is the traditional choice, though sometimes you can also get a whisky or cognac. In summer, a *limoncello*, delicious lemon liqueur from the Amalfi coast served ice cold, can be just the thing.

The Check

In polar opposition to the New York or Los Angeles hot spot that wants to hustle you out and "re-monetize" your table, Italian restaurants will rarely rush you to finish your meal. Indeed, you can sit there all night wondering what you have to do to get out of the place. It turns out the magic word is *conto* and you have to ask for it, since to bring it without your okay is considered rude.

COPERTO

The *coperto* is a traditional Italian cover charge that used to cover bread but now acts as a kind of pretip tip that gets added onto most restaurant bills. It usually comes to no more than a euro or two per person, though I have seen up to five. Take note that if the *coperto* is unusually high, you do not need to tip, as they've basically taken care of that for you.

Euroflation

In January 2002, the European Union introduced its spanking-new pan-European currency, the euro. Unencumbered by national boundaries or a long and troubled history, the euro symbolized a new beginning of cooperation and unity in Europe. Unfortunately, it also ushered in a wave of inflation that—at least in Italy—was overwhelming to locals and visitors alike. A drink or a plate of food that once cost 10,000 lire (about $5) suddenly cost €10 (around $10).

Things have leveled off a bit since the beginning, but Americans who travel to Florence may be surprised to find that a nice meal here costs the same as, or more than, a meal back home. A dinner for two plus wine at a casual trattoria can run about €50. A meal for two at a high-end restaurant can cost around €125.

Tipping

Tipping is one of those Italian mysteries for which it's difficult to get a straight answer. Some bills will say *servizio incluso*, in which case the restaurants have made the decision for you, but most don't. Do you need to leave a tip? "No, but . . . you can, if you want to," an Italian will tell you. If you are at a nice restaurant, you liked the service, and you don't see

Words to Shop By

Many of us are accustomed to browsing and shopping in silent anonymity, but here an exchange of greetings between buyer and seller is a customary part of all commerce. At first you may find it almost comical how Florentines insist on their stock civilities, but after a while you will grow to appreciate this token of friendly banter. Every time you enter a store, you should greet the owner with a hearty *buongiorno* or *buonasera*, depending on the time of day. When you buy your loot and go, you'll probably engage in a rally of *grazie* and *arrivederci*. You should never use the informal *ciao* in these situations, unless the person serving you is the same age you are or younger and gives hints of being a friendly, casual sort. But if and when anyone starts sending you off with *ciao*, feel free to say it back, especially as a final shout on the way out the door.

Other important shopping vocabulary:

Alimentari = General store selling basic food items

Bar = Primarily a casual place for a coffee or other drink, sometimes with a *panino*, *dolce*, or even a full meal

Forno = Bakery specializing in breads

Latteria = "Milk shop," typically a small market with a refrigerated case containing milk and packaged cheeses; usually also carries some packaged goods, such as pasta, cookies, coffee

Macelleria = Butcher shop

Mesticheria = General store selling kitchen and household supplies

Pasticceria = Shop selling pastries and cakes; sometimes also a *bar*

Pescheria = Fish shop

Pizzicheria = Store selling *salumi*, cheeses, and other assorted fresh and packaged foods, similar to *alimentari*

Polleria = Butcher shop specializing in poultry (they also sell beef, pork, and *salumi*)

Salumeria = *Pizzicheria* specializing in *salumi* (cold cuts)

service included on the bill, I would recommend just rounding up or leaving 10 percent in cash on the table, though it really is up to the diner's discretion.

Don't be surprised or offended by the occasional surly waiter or diffident salesperson—they do it to everyone, local and foreigner alike, particularly in the center of town. Remember, no one is working toward a tip, which makes a big difference in the quality in service. Of course, you will nearly as often encounter a shopkeeper or server so friendly, so helpful, that you'll forgive the Florentines their foibles, and their sometimes frosty attitude.

MARKETS AND SHOPS

The word *siesta* (or *pausa*, as the custom is known in Florence) rolls off your tongue like a lullaby, bringing to mind a world of Latin light and fun and long, sweet naps in the shade. Unfortunately, siesta has a darker side: stores close down in the afternoon year-round, usually from 1 PM to 5 PM. Many shops are also closed Monday mornings and Wednesday afternoons—though less commonly food stores—in addition to all day Sunday, because, well, they can. This means shopping for food, either in the morning or the evening, takes more advance planning than most of us are used to. It's certainly challenging and often annoying, but if the shopkeepers can hold the frantic workaholic world at bay for a while longer, I'm with them.

Coffee in Florence

I used to bait friends at home by saying that you can get a better cappuccino in the train station in Florence than you can in any café in San Francisco. I said it partly to provoke, but I'll stand by that claim: the cappuccino in the station bar is excellent (though the atmosphere is a tad hectic). It's hard to go wrong with coffee in Florence; in fact, there are so many great coffee bars that I haven't even tried to name most of them in this book. Is it the water, the machines, the cleaning of the machines, or a certain Italian *non so cosa* that makes every shot of coffee here like a little liquid rush of bliss? I can't tell you what a great pleasure and relief it is to a coffeehound like me to know that no matter where I am in Italy, from the far north to the deep south, from the biggest city to the smallest hamlet, I am almost never more than half a block from a good coffee.

But even in Italy, there's coffee and then there's coffee. The biggest name in local coffee roasting is **Piansa**, famous for its mix of arabica beans, but its main bar is far from the Center on the southeast side of town (Viale Europa 126–128r, 055/653-2117; open Monday through Friday 7 AM to 9 PM, Saturday and Sunday mornings). Luckily you can also buy Piansa coffee in the center of town at **Caffetteria Piansa** (Borgo Pinti 18r, 055/234-2362; open Monday through Saturday 8 AM to 8 PM) and **Cantinetta dei Verrazzano** (see page 48).

I had a rude awakening on my first visit to Italy when, fresh from the cafés of my California youth, I strolled into an Italian bar, asked for a *latte* and predictably was given a large glass of milk. So, it's a good idea to know your coffee vocabulary.

Caffè = Espresso

Caffè americano = Espresso with extra hot water added to resemble American coffee

Caffè corretto = Espresso with a shot of grappa or other liqueur or spirit

Caffè decaffeinato = Decaffeinated (also called Hag, pronounced "ahg")

Caffelatte = Hot milk with espresso, served in a glass

Caffè lungo = Same as *caffè americano*

Caffè macchiato = Espresso with a dollop of milk foam

Caffè shakerato = Sweet summertime drink of cold coffee and ice "shaken" and served in a cocktail glass

Cappuccino = Espresso with hot milk and foam

Latte = Glass of milk

Latte macchiato = Hot milk with a dollop of espresso

Tè = Tea

Tè deteinato = Decaffeinated tea

The center of Florence is blissfully walkable. You can reach most sites and businesses in the narrow alleyways of the Center more easily on foot (or bike) than by any kind of motorized transport. But when you're out and about, or want to explore the periphery and perhaps aren't in the mood for an hour-long walk, there are a few things you should know.

Florentine Addresses

With a few exceptions, residential addresses in Florence are big and blue and business addresses are smaller and red. When an address reads "Via della Condotta 26r," the r refers to red. This causes confusion because streets will have two of each address number, one blue, one red.

Taking the Bus

Florence has two bus systems, the small lettered electric buses (A through D) that cover the center of town, and the bigger buses, numbered 1 through 80-something, that spread out and cover an impressive area in every direction from the Center, from Scandicci to Sesto Fiorentino. It's helpful to have a bus map, either from the ATAF (the bus company) office in front of the train station or from a tourist office. The map not only shows you all the bus routes but is also just a good map of the city. Before you get on a bus, you'll need to buy a ticket, which you can do at any *tabaccheria* or any bar displaying the ATAF sticker on its window. If you plan to use the bus regularly, consider buying a *biglietto multiplo*, which gives you four rides at a slight discount. Once on a bus, validate your ticket by sticking it in one of the yellow machines. The buses work on an honor system and most of the time no one will check your ticket, but if you get caught without one, or with a ticket that hasn't been validated, you'll get a hefty fine.

Most bus lines lead to and from the central train station and branch out from there. Piazza San Marco and Piazza Antinori are two other hubs. You may find yourself using the station as either a starting point or transfer point for many of your voyages. Bus service becomes *much* less frequent after about 9 PM, so if you take a bus to dinner at a restaurant, you might find yourself taking a taxi back to where you are staying.

Service on Sunday is also less frequent than during the week. At most bus stops, you'll find schedules for the various buses that stop there. They are more or less accurate and will tell you when the buses cease running for the day.

As this second edition goes to press, the construction of Florence's new tramlines is in full swing, though the work is also running behind schedule. When finished, the lines will mostly be useful for commuters who are traveling from the Florentine suburbs, like Scandicci, into the center, rather than for visitors who are staying in the historic core for a few days.

Taking a Taxi

Taxi drivers in Florence prefer to be called rather than hailed. If you see a taxi stand, then by all means go for it, but otherwise your best bet is to call. Your hotel, if you have one, can call for you, of course, as will any restaurant. The main taxi line is **Radio Taxi: 055/4242**, and the beautiful thing is, once you call them, they come immediately. Taxis here tend to be clean and new, and the drivers are often knowledgable and sometimes even friendly. Taxi rides become more expensive after 9 PM, if you have baggage, and if your party has more than two people. Tipping is not expected, though you can round up if you feel like it. Most cabs will only take a maximum of four people, but if you tell them you are five when you call, they will send a larger car.

The Listings in This Book

The overall organization of the book is by neighborhood, a change made for the second edition. Within each chapter, the listings are divided by type, first restaurants and trattorias, then pizzerias, then wine bars, and so on. The listings are then arranged alphabetically, or as alphabetically as possible. Finally, pricing information is given only for restaurants and trattorias and is noted along with the rest of the service information at the top of each listing. Keep in mind that prices do and will change and are also highly variable depending on what you order. The pricing key for the book is as follows:

Inexpensive, € = Under €20 per person including wine and *coperto*

Moderately priced, €€ = From €20 to €45

Expensive, €€€ = From €45 to €75

Very expensive, €€€€ = €75 and up

For several reasons, alphabetizing in Italian is tricky, as a glance through the Florence phonebook bears out. Trattoria Mario might be listed under *T*, *M*, neither, or both. I have tried to alphabetize in a way that is both loyal to Italian grammar and rational to an English-speaking user. To this end, I have omitted the nominal designation of a place (trattoria, gelateria, ristorante) in the listing unless it is an integral part of the name.

Most listings include a map designation (for example, D4) that refers to the map on pages 224 and 225. When a location falls outside the map, I have indicated the neighborhood or town.

A star (✳) next to a listing means that the spot is exceptional—a personal favorite.

1

THE REGIONAL FOODS OF FLORENCE AND TUSCANY

Like the light gray *pietra serena* stone from the outlying hills that makes up the backbone of distinctive Florentine architecture, the abundant raw ingredients of Tuscany form the foundation for its hearty traditional dishes. The regional gastronomy is identifiable by its simplicity and quality, with a clear distaste for anything too fussy and fancy. Here is a brief list of ingredients and dishes that are unmistakably Tuscan.

BEANS

You'll find them in most Tuscan soups, and as a side dish either plain or sautéed seasoned with garlic and tomatoes. Beans (*fagioli*) are an integral part of the Tuscan diet: they are inexpensive, healthful, and delicious—especially when handled with expertise, as the Florentine cooks do. Small white beans, called *toscanelli* by Florentines, are the most popular. They turn up in *ribollita*, in *pasta e fagioli* (thick bean soup with pasta), and often as a side dish to roasted meats and poultry. You'll also come across plenty of chickpeas (*ceci*) used in the primo *pasta e ceci* (similar to *pasta e fagioli*, but with *ceci* and a taste of rosemary) and elsewhere.

Far rarer, but worth seeking out, is the *zolfino* bean, a regional specialty that sells for almost thirty euros per pound. The small, butter-colored legumes, which are grown only in a slim, steep valley near Arezzo, are prized for their creamy consistency and thin skin. You can find them dried at the **Central** and **Sant'Ambrogio** markets (see pages 100 and 89, respectively) and at **Morganti** in Piazza Santo Spirito (see page 125), and occasionally on the menus of fine restaurants.

Bistecca alla Fiorentina

A few years ago, a dark pall fell over the city of Florence. No, it was not a sequel to the plague that drove Boccaccio to flee the city in the Middle Ages. Fears about a more modern scourge, mad cow disease (called *mucca pazza* in Italian), led the European Union to outlaw the sale and consumption of beef on the bone, including the beloved premier dish of Florence, *bistecca alla fiorentina*. I am happy to say that it's now back on the menu—in fact you can find it at almost every restaurant in town.

The origins of *bistecca alla fiorentina* are a bit murky, but the name was supposedly coined by traveling Englishmen happy to see a juicy, familiar "beefsteak" on their table. A *fiorentina* is simply the T-bone cut (often enormous, enough to serve two), about one and a half inches thick, grilled over charcoal or wood and always served rare, with just olive oil, salt, and occasionally lemon or rosemary for flavoring. (Asking for a *fiorentina* well done is like asking a sushi chef to microwave your tuna roll.) When a *fiorentina* is cooked properly, it tastes tender and juicy, and though it is rare, it doesn't taste raw. This is Florentine cooking at its simple and flavorful best.

Locals believe that the most flavorful, tender beef in all of Europe comes from white-coated, grass-fed Chianina cattle, which are raised in the Val di Chiana area, around Siena and Arezzo, and in the Mugello area. The beef has become very expensive, however, and most *bistecche* around town are not from Chianina cattle (if they are, the menu will say so). Chianina beef is also something of an acquired taste, and regular grass-fed Tuscan beef may taste just as satisfying.

Some of the best places in town to sample *bistecca alla fiorentina*:

All' Antico Ristoro di Cambi, *page 126*

Trattoria Mario, *page 94*

Omero, *page 146*

Osvaldo, *page 148*

Vecchia Bettola, *page 132*

The Mushroom Season

If you are lucky enough to be in Florence in fall (one of the most beautiful times of the year here), you should take advantage of some of the seasonal delicacies. In October and November, Florence and the rest of Tuscany offer a bounty of fresh wild mushrooms that can be difficult—or impossible—to find elsewhere. Foragers bring surprisingly large "harvests" of porcini, *galletti*, and other excellent fungi to the city's produce markets. Look for mushrooms that say *nostrali* (locally grown). For the prized black and white truffles from Piedmont and some points closer, you need to wait until later in November. You will find the mushrooms in the best produce markets, and they also pop up on some menus, adorning a plate of tagliatelle, brushed with olive oil and grilled, or stuffed for an appetizer.

Porcini

Part of the boletus family, porcini are probably the best known mushrooms of the bunch. They are stocky, with a stem almost as wide as the head. You will see them sold alongside a peculiar herb called *nepitella*. Sometimes translated as catamint, *nepitella* recalls thyme with a hint of mint and is considered the natural partner for porcini. Sauté the porcini and *nepitella* with garlic and a little white wine for a great pasta sauce.

Galletti

These delicate-looking yellowish mushrooms turn up around the same time as porcini. They look and even taste a little like chanterelles, with a fragrance reminiscent of apricots and a slightly acidic edge. Florentines like to sauté them with garlic and parsley or add them to a frittata, always being careful not to overpower their delicate flavor.

Ovoli

Another fall find, these unusual funghi have big, white stems and huge, bright yellow heads that make them look a little sinister. In fact, they are closely related to some poisonous mushrooms. But if you see them at the market, take a chance. Ovoli can be sliced and eaten raw in salads or cooked on a grill as you would a portobello.

CAVOLO NERO

Along with beans, bread, wine, and oil, *cavolo nero*, a dark, crinkly, long-stalked winter green, is a staple of the Florentine kitchen. Literally "black cabbage," *cavolo nero* is in fact most similar to a variety of kale known as dinosaur (or *lacinato*) kale. It is the signature vegetable of Tuscany, forming the backbone of *ribollita* and also satisfying—and popular—when boiled in salted water and then sautéed with garlic and oil. I've had it as a simple side dish and also as a topping for crostini over melted pecorino cheese. The long, glorious culinary life that Florentines have given their *cavolo nero* illustrates their pluck: where others would see a bitter, funny-looking plant, they uncovered vegetal gold.

LARDO DI COLONNATA

In the first edition of this book, I felt that I had to introduce readers to the joys of *lardo*, as pork fat was, at the time, anathema to the contemporary American diet. But now, with Mario Batali having made Manhattan into the fifth borough of Tuscany and Emilia-Romagna, *lardo* is no longer unknown or feared.

Lardo di Colonnata is not like grandma's baking lard, but instead a prized delicacy. The town of Colonnata, close to Carrara, is famous for both its beautiful white marble and its *lardo*. Here, a small number of dedicated producers cure pork fat with salt and herbs and age it in special marble tubs. Try *lardo* if you see it listed as an antipasto. Sliced thin and served warm on crostini, it simply melts in your mouth, giving you a whole new perspective on pork fat.

OLIO DI OLIVA EXTRAVIRGINE

In Tuscany, where oil production dates back to the Etruscans, extra virgin olive oil greases the gears of life. The region's ubiquitous olive trees, with their thin, silverish leaves, provide about 20 percent of Italy's oil. The peppery, greenish gold oil is the Tuscan universal solvent, as appreciated and venerated as fine wine. It gets tossed with wild greens, poured over hot soups and pastas, and dripped on hot bread to make the regional version of bruschetta, called *fettunta* (roughly translated as "oiled slice").

Easy Being Green

If you have access to a kitchen in Florence, try experimenting with
some of the wonderful greens—wild and cultivated—that flourish in
the region. During fall and winter, at the **Central** and **Sant'Ambrogio**
markets (see pages 100 and 89, respectively), at the farmers' stalls
such as those at **Piazza Santo Spirito** every morning, and the **Cascine
Market** (see page 161) on Tuesdays, you can find all kinds of dark,
leafy greens and lettuces. At first, the piles of mysterious vegetation
can be a little intimidating, but if you take the time to find out what
they are and how to eat them, you'll be richly rewarded. In addition to
cavolo nero, try the long, spiky *puntarelle* (chicory), the bitter *cima di
rape* (turnip greens), and wild borage and other greens. You'll also
find a fine lettuce called *delicata*, delicious escarole, and several kinds
of chard (*bietola*). The more tender greens can be eaten raw in salad
with a little salt, lemon juice, and olive oil, and nearly all of them can

be blanched and then
sautéed with garlic and
hot pepper flakes and
served as a side dish to
roast pork or beef. They
can also be mixed with
sausage for a pasta
sauce or simmered in a
bean soup. The fresh-
ness and variety of the
greens in Florentine
markets are enough to
make anyone eat his or
her vegetables with
gusto.

Tuscans are so fond of their strong-flavored oil that they even use it for deep-frying and occasionally for baking and desserts. As Cristina Blasi of Florence's Cordon Bleu cooking school put it, "For us Tuscans, other oils simply don't exist." Mothers even use it to cure their babies' diaper rash.

In late October and November, the olives are either painstakingly picked by hand or harvested mechanically (some growers use a machine that vibrates the tree, sending the olives into large nets at the base). Once the olives get to the mill, which must happen immediately after they're picked, they are cleaned and then the whole fruit—pit, meat, and skin—is crushed to a pulp between large stones. The pulp is either spread on nylon mats interspersed with stainless-steel disks (the traditional method) or, more common now, centrifuged to separate the oil from the water. The oil is kept for up to a month in large steel containers, during which the debris settles to the bottom, and then the oil is clarified and ready for the final stage, filtration. The result is green-tinted, fresh-tasting extra virgin olive oil.

Tuscans consume so much oil that they actually import olives from other countries, usually Spain and Greece, to meet local demand. If you want to ensure the olives are local, look for estate-bottled oils that say *prodotto e imbottigliato nel*, followed by the name of the estate. You can expect to pay ten to twenty-five euros for an estate-grown and bottled liter. It's not cheap, but the cost makes sense when you consider that it takes five kilograms (about ten pounds) of olives to make one liter of extra virgin oil. However, if you don't need a name-brand estate on the label, you can buy less fancy and still delicious extra virgin oil for far less money.

Extra virgin means that the oil comes from the first pressing and has less than 1 percent acidity, and has also been officially tasted to assure the best flavor. There is really no reason to buy anything other than extra virgin, though some people believe it's better to fry in regular (virgin) olive oil so as not to waste money. The finest estate-bottled oils are best used raw, drizzled on top of vegetables and soups, to grasp their flavor fully, though you can certainly cook with them, too. I like to keep one bottle of inexpensive extra virgin and one smaller bottle of finer oil in the house so that I'm prepared for any culinary need.

Cultivation of grapevines and olive trees often goes hand in hand, so it's not surprising that some of the best oils come from estates known for their wines. Among them are Badia a Coltibuono, Querciabella, Castello di Ama, and Capezzana, to name only a few.

PANE TOSCANO

You never realize how important a touch of salt is to bread until you taste bread made without it, otherwise known as *pane toscano* (Tuscan bread). But Tuscans will vigorously defend their saltless bread. Traditionally, this peasant bread is made with coarse flour and wild natural yeast and baked in a wood-fired oven, though you will rarely find it in this pure form nowadays. The absence of salt causes the bread to form a thicker, dusty pale brown crust. Tuscans claim that the organic yeastlike organisms trapped inside the usually large (one kilogram/two pounds or more)

Saltless and salted bread on sale.

loaves make the bread easier to digest and also make it last longer, which was important in the days when the method was invented.

By itself, Tuscan bread tastes dry and dull to a foreign palate, but there are times when it is just the thing: for sopping up the salty sauce of a meat dish (which locals call *fare la scarpetta*, or "doing the slipper") or adding to a flavorful soup. Bread is also a key ingredient in several ubiquitous Tuscan dishes, including *ribollita*, *pappa al pomodoro*, and *panzanella*.

If you want to order bread with salt in a bakery, you can ask either for *pane salato* or *pane pugliese*. I am trying to develop the taste for Tuscan bread, though I am finding it tough going. And then I have to wonder, if Tuscans love their traditional bread so much, why is the salted bread at the bakery always sold out?

Some places to find good Tuscan and other breads:

Forno Galli, *Via S. Agostino 8r, 055/219-703*

Forno Pagnotti, *Borgo La Croce 109r, 055/247-9362*

Forno Sartoni, *page 50*

Cantinetta dei Verrazzano, *page 48*

PECORINO TOSCANO

Outside of Italy, when people think of pecorino they usually think of hard, aged Pecorino Romano, which is often grated onto pasta as a substitute for the more expensive Parmesan. Pecorino Toscano in its various forms has not yet made serious inroads into the export market, but it's certainly popular among the locals. Pecorino is made from sheep's milk and aged for varying amounts of time, from twenty days for soft and mild pecorino fresco to several months for the deliciously tart, medium-density, semiaged (*mezzo-stagionato*) or aged (*stagionato*) versions, which goes well with pears, green apples, and Chianti wine.

Experts claim the fine taste of Tuscan pecorino is due to the region's excellent grassy grazing areas. Its manufacture was already regulated as far back as the nineteenth century, but the cheese didn't receive its prestigious DOP (protected designation of origin) status until 1986. It's still one of only about two dozen cheeses with the DOP label. The skin is usually a soft yellow, unless it has been tinted with ash or dried tomato, and the inside is a buttery white. The rounds typically weigh between one and three kilograms (two and six pounds). Pecorino from Pienza Province is especially prized (you'll sometimes see it named on menus) and comes in smaller rounds. It is aged from two to six months, yielding results that range from a soft, fairly mild "eating cheese" to a semiaged product with a definite kick.

RIBOLLITA

What began life as a peasant soup made from leftovers has become one of the signature dishes of Florence. *Ribollita*, a thick mix of beans, bread, and *cavolo nero* (see page 20), will warm you up in winter more effectively than a down parka. It is made by preparing a *soffritto* of carrot, celery, and onion to which beans (sometimes puréed), stale bread, and *cavolo nero* are added. You can make it at home, but it is never quite as enjoyable as eating it at the local trattoria, where it usually arrives in a thick ceramic bowl (to retain the heat) and is accompanied with a glass of Chianti or Morellino di Scansano. Some of the best places to find a good bowl of *ribollita*:

Osteria Antica Mescita di San Niccolò, *page 136*

Trattoria Mario, *page 94*

Da Ruggiero, *page 149*

Vecchia Bettola, *page 132*

SALUMI TOSCANI

Tuscan *salumi* are known and appreciated throughout Italy, and they turn up as a specialty on menus from Venice to Palermo. The prosciutto, salami, and other cured meats of this area tend to be salty and strong flavored. Tuscans love their cold cuts and usually eat prosciutto and pancetta plain, with no need for bread as an intermediary.

Prosciutto toscano: Perhaps not as famous as its counterpart from Parma, Tuscan prosciutto—a dry-cured leg of raw ham, aged for at least a year—is salty, delicious, and subtly flavored with a mix of rosemary, garlic, pepper, and juniper berries. Prosciutto production in Tuscany is limited, which means you'll be hard-pressed to find it outside Italy. The local prosciutto is referred to as "salato," as opposed to the "dolce" style that comes from Parma and elsewhere. If you ask for *prosciutto toscano*, *salato*, or *casalingo*, you will get the same thing.

Pancetta: Italian-style bacon that is salt-cured instead of smoked, pancetta isn't a specialty of Tuscany, but it is prevalent here. You usually see it in a wide bricklike piece topped with lots of pepper.

Salame toscano: This all-pork salami is made with lots of pepper, spices, and a fair amount of fat. It is great in sandwiches and is an excellent all-around salami.

Finocchiona: Larger than a *salame toscano*, *finocchiona* is made of coarsely chopped pork, pork fat, and fennel seeds, stuffed in a natural casing. It's a specialty of the area around Prato.

Soppressata: This headcheese, or pig's head sausage, is made from left-over pieces of meat and cartilage and is flavored with salt, pepper, garlic, and lemon peel. It's not to everyone's liking, but it can be very good when made by an artisanal producer and sliced thin.

Cinta Senese salumi: Cinta Senese refers to a rare breed of free-range pig—named for the white pelt that encircles the animal's front quarters and looks like a belt, or *cinta*—raised in the hills outside Siena. These special swine get to roam through the forest and eat twigs and leaves and acorns instead of the banal slop fed to their penned cousins. This results in an especially dark, fatty, and flavorful meat, made into pancetta, prosciutto, salami, and *guanciale* (cured cheek meat). Because the breed is feisty and hard to raise, production is small and the meat is extremely costly, up to fifty euros per kilogram (two pounds).

Prosciutto e salame di cinghiale: Wild boar roam primarily in the Maremma area in southern Tuscany, as well as near Arezzo, and are a favorite catch for hunters. The dark, gamey meat can be made into salami, prosciutto, and sausage. These products have a strong, distinctive flavor, are a bit greasy, and go better with cheese and bread than on their own.

SCHIACCIATA

Schiacciata is a multifaceted word. When a friend broke her hand and went to the hospital, the doctor's diagnosis was *schiacciata*. How do you want your nuts from the store, whole or *schiacciata*? When Kobe Bryant makes a slam dunk at the all-star game, what do the announcers yell: *Schiacciataaaaa! Schiacciata*, pronounced skee-ah-cha-ta, essentially means crushed, broken, squashed, or slammed, though when you're hungry, the most important definition is a perfect rectangle of salty, golden focaccia-like bread. It is Florence's answer to Ligurian focaccia, which is higher and airier. To make it, the bakers take the dough for *pane toscano*, flatten it into a sheet, poke it with their fingers, and top it with a hefty dose of salt and oil before baking. The result is a delicious snack, often crowned with onions, anchovies, or various other savories. Florentine babies and kids cry out for it, though sometimes they can only get out "cha cha"; it's okay, their parents know what they want. For first-rate *schiacciata*, stop at Pugi (see page 97) or any reliable *forno* (bakery) in town.

Wines by the glass at Fratellini.

2

A Primer
on Tuscan Wine

From Fiasco to Forerunner

For most people, Tuscan wine means Chianti, but this fertile region produces an impressive and sometimes overwhelming list of wines, from light whites that go down easily to full-bodied Brunello di Montalcino, which pairs well with a heavy meal to counter its bold personality. Even so, multifaceted and highly drinkable Chianti Classico is number one here, and the traditional Sangiovese grape still reigns as big grape.

In the 1970s and early 1980s, Chianti wine hit a low point in its long history. Coasting on its famed appellation, the producers put out more and more wine of decreasing quality, much of it diluted by a large percentage of white grapes. Chianti's reputation suffered, and its wines became synonymous with the cheap, watery stuff usually sold in the bulbous, straw-laced bottle ironically called a *fiasco*.

Fortunately, a group of dedicated winegrowers decided to take matters into their own hands and raise standards of Tuscan wine to compete in international markets with France and the New World. Taking cues from the French in particular, these forward-thinking winery owners and their hardworking oenologists began experimenting with growing Cabernet Sauvignon and Merlot grapes to add to their reds, Chardonnay and Sauvignon Blanc to spice up the whites, and importing French oak *barriques*—smaller than the more traditional large Slavic barrels—to impart an oakier flavor to the wines as they age. Even more important, the winemakers put enormous resources into their core product by improving the quality of their Sangiovese grapes and replanting entire vineyards. The result of all this work, which often fell outside the DOC and DOCG regulations (see box, opposite), was both the advent of the Supertuscan and a vast improvement in Chianti Classico. Because of changes in DOC regulations, most so-called Supertuscans now have either IGT or DOC status. And Chianti Classico, far from the fiasco it once was, now rarely sells for less than ten euros a bottle, and often much more.

DECIPHERING THE WINE LIST

Because the euro-to-dollar exchange rate has favored the euro for the last few years, the Italian wine industry has had a hard time exporting wine to the United States. While in Florence and the surrounding area, take the opportunity to taste wines made by small producers, white wines, and dessert wines that you simply can't find at home.

Chianti Classico

Chianti Classico refers to the heart of the Chianti region, the rolling hills between Florence and Siena, which includes the towns of Greve, Radda, Castellina, Gaiole, and parts of other territories. There is no doubt that some of Tuscany's finest and certainly most characteristic wines— epitomizing the Tuscan *terroir*, somewhat dry as far as red wines go, with hints of raspberry and cherry and a slight kick—come from this area. Chianti Classico wine is traditionally made from Sangiovese grapes, with a small addition of Canaiolo, Colorino, or other complementary grapes. Now you can find DOCG Chianti Classico wines that have Sangiovese mixed with Cabernet Sauvignon, with Merlot, or even made of 100 percent Sangiovese, which ironically used to be verboten.

A wine labeled Chianti Classico *riserva* has been aged longer than regular Chianti—sometimes in oak barrels—and has a higher alcohol content and usually a smoother texture and deeper flavor. It also costs a bit more. Some of the names to look out for in both the *riserva* and regular Classico categories are Fonterutoli, Fontodi, Querciabella, Castello di Brolio, Isole e Olena, and Castell'in Villa. Castello di Ama and Felsina also turn out top-quality, special-occasion Chiantis, while Castello Aiola and Villa Vistarenni make some good low-priced bottles.

What's Up, DOC?

You may have already attempted to unscramble the acronyms adorning your bottle of Chianti or Vernaccia. Many flaunt the DOC or DOCG labels, which stand for *Denominazione d' Origine Controllata* and—even better—*Denominazione d' Origine Controllata e Garantita*, respectively. (The DOCG is simply a stricter version of DOC, with tighter guidelines and higher standards.) The DOC system (pronounced "doc," not "d.o.c.") is Italy's answer to the French appellation system, in which wines are regulated under strict guidelines by the government. DOC regulations affect everything from the grape varietals allowed (including specific percentages) to yield and aging, all pegged to a geographical growing area. In order to earn their DOC stripes in Tuscany, wines must follow the regulations and then be tasted and approved by elected officials in Florence and Siena.

Most of all, as the name implies, the DOC label is a guarantee that your Chianti Rufina really comes from the Rufina area. This is important, since Italian wines are known primarily by geographical origin—tied intrinsically to their *terroir*—rather than by grape (for example, Chianti is called Chianti, not Sangiovese). What can you take away from all of this? Essentially, these acronyms are an assurance of consistency and quality. They don't promise that you'll like the wine, but they are a decent indication that someone knew what he or she was doing when it was made. In other words, it's not necessary to have the DOC label, but as an authoritative marker in the sea of wines, it helps.

Vino Nobile, Brunello di Montalcino, and Vernaccia of San Gimigniano were among the first DOC wines in Italy. In the mid-1980s, the central Chianti Classico region was raised from DOC to DOCG, tightening guidelines, eliminating some of the shoddy practices previously in place, and generally helping raise the status of Chianti wines. Recently, not only Chianti Classico and the other traditional leaders but also Colli Senesi, Colli Aretini, Rufina, Colli Fiorentini (all wines from the hills around Florence, Siena, and Arezzo), and a handful of other Tuscan wines have been graced with the DOCG denomination.

Most non-DOC wines are now marked IGT, for *Indicazione Geografica Tipica*. The IGT label is a way of identifying that someone is experimenting outside the DOC system, yet the wine has been tasted and certified by the authorities. Although it is becoming less common, you will occasionally see a bottle marked simply *vino da tavola* (table wine). This means that the wine is made completely outside the denomination system and implies that it uses grapes grown outside its own geographic area—for example, cheaper "blending" grapes from Puglia or Sicily. In the 1980s and into the 1990s, the original Supertuscans were labeled *vino da tavola*, but you rarely see that on a fine bottle now, so the phrase has reverted to its original meaning: basic.

On some bottles of Chianti Classico, in addition to the DOCG appellation, you'll see a logo of a black rooster, representing the Gallo Nero. This consortium of Chianti Classico winemakers is purely voluntary and promotional, so again, it's not a guarantee of anything in particular, but it is a stamp of peer approval.

Other Chiantis

The greater Chianti winemaking region comprises the provinces of Florence, Arezzo, Siena, Pisa, and Pistoia. Don't be afraid to venture outside Chianti Classico for your bottle of wine. Vintages from Chianti Rufina, Colli Senesi, and Colli Fiorentini have also improved over the past few years (Rufina is generally agreed to yield the finest wines) and tend to be economical. They can be drunk quite young but are at their best when aged one to four years. Names to look for include Frescobaldi, Colognole, Lanciola, and La Querce.

Carmignano

In the small winemaking area around Carmignano, winemakers have been adding Cabernet Sauvignon to their Sangiovese before it was even a trend and thus set themselves apart from the Chianti region. This area west of Florence encompasses Artimino, Carmignano, and Poggio a Caiano (for more on this area, see page 174). Current DOCG regulations now stipulate nearly two years of aging, and 45 to 70 percent Sangiovese, with the rest a mix of Cabernet and other grapes, at the discretion of the individual maker. The name that comes up most often in respect to Carmignano is Tenuta di Capezzana, though other good wines come from Villa Artimino, Fattoria Baccheretto, and Fattoria Il Poggiolo. Capezzana and other producers also put out a lighter, less expensive DOC red called Barco Reale and a popular rosé called Vin Ruspo.

Bolgheri and the Maremma

This region on the Maremma coast of Tuscany, south of Pisa, is a winemaking hot spot. Every big producer from Piedmont to Puglia wants to stake a claim in this fertile coastal soil. In fact, the Bolgheri denomination could be supplanting Brunello as the region's most prestigious. The area's reputation as prime grape-growing territory can be traced to Tenuta San Guido's introduction of Sassicaia, the original Supertuscan, in 1968. In 2001, *Wine Spectator* chose Tenuta dell'Ornellaia's Bolgheri Superiore Ornellaia as its wine of the year, and in 2002 Ornellaia was sold to a partnership that includes the Frescobaldi family and Robert Mondavi of California.

As this one-time boggy, mosquito-filled zone has become widely acknowledged as a winemaking paradise, Bolgheri has been given several DOC denominations, including Bolgheri Rosso and Bolgheri Bianco; plus, Sassicaia became the first single-vineyard DOC in all of Italy. The Bolgheri reds are characterized by their use of "international" grapes, which grow so well here. They are usually made using a majority of Cabernet Sauvignon, Cabernet Franc, or Merlot. With popularity and hype come high prices, however, and the name Bolgheri on a bottle sometimes entails a steep price, especially for the top wines of San Guido and Ornellaia. (For more information on this region and its wines, see page 196.)

In addition to the big names like Guado al Tasso and Ornellaia, several small producers are creating excellent wines that are accessible and complex even when young. Among the smaller, less expensive but eminently drinkable wines of this area are those made by Enrico Santini: an excellent low-priced red called Poggio al Moro, a more sophisticated Bolgheri Superiore, and a light *bianco* made mostly of Trebbiano grapes. And producer Michele Satta is gaining popularity for his drinkable reds and whites.

In an ever-expanding wave of wine appreciation, the nearby region of Val di Cornia and even the island of Elba have been granted their own DOC status. The Val di Cornia includes the area around Suvereto, where some of the labels to look for are Tua Rita, Le Pinacce, and Jacopo Banti.

Morellino di Scansano

Now that Chianti Classico has become relatively fine and expensive, this affordable, drinkable red wine could be in position to assume its

Bottles on display at Millesimi.

place as the every-night dinner wine of Tuscany. It hails from Scansano in the Maremma region, just southeast of Bolgheri. Morellino is a variant of the Sangiovese grape and is sometimes blended with Malvasia Nera, Canaiolo, or Grenache. Like Chianti, Morellino di Scansano has a bright ruby color and plenty of body, but not so much as to overpower your meal. Some good choices in this category are Moris Farms, Il Boscheto, and Erik Banti, who is often credited with spearheading the comeback of this wine region. Plenty of estates such as Fonterutoli and Rocca delle Macie, better known for their Chianti Classicos, have also staked a claim here and begun to make their own Morellino.

Brunello and Rosso di Montalcino

The sloping hillsides around Montalcino capture the postcard fantasy of green and sunny Tuscany. The Brunello grape, also called Sangiovese Grosso, has been grown here for more than a century, giving local winemakers plenty of time to perfect their craft. To be considered Brunello di Montalcino, among other requirements, the wine must be made from 100 percent Sangiovese Grosso, and it must age for a minimum of four years (two years in oak)—five years for a *riserva*—after which it is vigorously taste-tested. Usually the wine ages in a combination of Slavic *botti*, or large barrels, and smaller *barriques*, until just the right flavor is achieved. The robust result pairs well with such big-flavored dishes as hearty winter roasts. To get some of the taste of Brunello without the punch—or the price, which is always high—try a Rosso di Montalcino, made from the same grape but with less stringent requirements and aged for a much shorter time. Poggio di Sotto, La Poderina, Siro Pacenti, and Col d'Orcia all produce award-winning Brunellos. Villa Banfi, Castelgiocondo, Fattoria Barbi, and Biondi-Santi are some of the best-known producers in the region, consistently making excellent wines.

Vino Nobile and Rosso di Montepulciano

Vino Nobile is like Brunello's younger brother: the same prestigious pedigree, the same depth of flavor, but literally younger—made from a minimum of 70 percent Sangiovese grapes and aged for three years instead of four—so it is usually a touch lighter and less expensive. Also like Brunello, Vino Nobile's grapes enjoy prime real estate on southern Tuscany's sun-drenched hillsides. Swept up in the tide of Tuscan wine's renewal, Nobile has undergone improvements in the past ten years, helped by dedicated vintners such as Poliziano and Avignonesi. Nobile also has its own more accessible line of Rossos priced for everyday consumption and extremely satisfying on their own merits. (Don't confuse these wines with Montepulciano d'Abruzzo, an unrelated wine from the Abruzzo region.) In addition to Poliziano and Avignonesi, look for excellent Nobiles from Fattoria del Cerro, Tenuta Valdipiatta, and Villa Sant'Anna.

Supertuscans and IGT Wines

Tenuta San Guido's Sassicaia and Antinori's Tignanello launched a revolution in Tuscan winemaking in the 1970s and early 1980s that still reverberates today. The term *Supertuscan* was coined in the 1980s by American wine writers who were bowled over by the new Tuscan *vini da tavola*. But they didn't want these top wines to be confused with regular table wine, hence the superlative new name, which was eagerly embraced by Italians (who pronounce it "Soopertooscan"), and the winemakers themselves, who couldn't have come up with a better marketing tool. The wines, which were originally made outside the DOC and DOCG restrictions, were mainly distinguished by two things: their use of such international grapes as Cabernet Sauvignon, Cabernet Franc, and Merlot, either alone or mixed with native Sangiovese; and aging in small French oak *barriques*. The term *Supertuscan* has started to fall out of use in recent times, partly because almost all of these wines are now covered under either the IGT or DOC umbrella.

The IGT designation (see page 31) allows winemakers more freedom and creativity, while still giving an assurance of quality and guarantee of *terroir*. So a beautifully made red wine that mixes Sangiovese with international grapes, is made in a valley close to Siena, and has a designer label and a funny name like Fortunaia would have been a Supertuscan in the past, but now usually carries an IGT label (unless it falls under a recently established DOC—confused yet?). Whereas the so-called Supertuscans were almost all high-priced wines, IGT is used for less expensive wines that fall outside the DOCs. Go figure. There are many many excellent IGT wines on the market, however, in every price range. On the high end, a few to look out for include Siepi from Fonterutoli, Giusto di Nostri from the Tua Rita estate, Felsina's classic Supertuscan Fontalloro, and 50 & 50 from Avignonesi and Capanelle. For lower-priced but still excellent bottles, keep an eye out for anything from the producer Bullichella, a delicious and affordable Sangiovese-based wine called Casamatta, and Il Nero di Casanova, which is 100% Sangiovese.

Vino Novello

It was inevitable that winemakers looking north toward France would also want to try their hand at *vini novelli* (new wines), an Italian version of Beaujolais Nouveau. The trend began in the northern regions of the Veneto and Friuli, but Tuscans are also getting in on it. Like Beaujolais, the *vini novelli* are made using the carbonic maceration process, which ferments the just-pressed grapes in such a way that the wine can forgo traditional aging. It also conveniently allows the wineries to off-load some of the wine they would normally age in expensive barrels, earning them some cash in what is usually a downtime of the year.

Every November brings the clamorous announcements of the arrival of the *novelli*, with bottles often costing less than five euros. In my opinion, these wines have yet to hit their stride. Instead of being light, fruity drinkable reds, many fall flat. It's likely, given their track record for success, that the dogged Tuscan winemakers will soon produce bright red *novelli* that are pleasing to everyone. Some producers making *vini novelli* are Antinori, Villa Banfi, and Rocca delle Macie.

Whites Wines

Although Tuscany is best known for its ruby red wines, local winemakers, eyes turned toward California and France, have been creating some internationally acclaimed whites, increasingly by using tried-and-true imported grapes, such as Chardonnay and Sauvignon Blanc, rather than the local white grapes, the less-exciting Trebbiano and Malvasia. These refined, sometimes oak-aged bottles are the present and, it seems, the future of white wine in Tuscany, competing with the traditional proud whites from farther north in Piedmont and Friuli. Castello di Ama makes an extremely aromatic Chardonnay that is so oaky it might not be to everyone's liking. Bolgheri winemakers such as Ornellaia, Enrico Santini, and Michele Satta all turn out decidedly lighter whites that go well with light meals.

San Gimignano's Vernaccia was one of the first wines in Italy to be granted DOC status. The Vernaccia grape creates a dry, full-bodied white and is sometimes mixed with a small amount of other grapes, usually Malvasia or Trebbiano. The storied wine has had its ups and downs but has come back fairly strong, thanks to the confident care of several key makers, including Tenuta Le Calcinaie, La Lastra, and Giovanni Panizzi. Vernaccia is one of the only traditional whites to retain its popularity in today's market, while everyone else is going Chardonnay. Other whites have evolved over the past ten years, including Bianco di Pitigliano, Bianco Vergine Valdichiana, and refined whites from the Montecarlo region.

Vin Santo

Instead of dessert, many Florentines opt for a plate of crunchy *cantucci* (also called *biscotti* or *biscottini*) and a glass of amber *vin santo* (literally, "holy wine") for dipping. *Vin santo* is usually made from Malvasia and/or Trebbiano grapes that, instead of rotting on the trees à la Sauternes, are either dried out on mats or hung from a ceiling for a period of weeks before spending the next six to ten years in small oak barrels. The process, which is lengthy and costly, results in a small output of delicious dessert wine that is either sweet or dry, depending on small variances in its creation. Not surprisingly, this prized drink is usually quite expensive. You'll find many bottles labeled *vin santo* marked at under ten euros per liter, but this is not true *vin santo*. It is fortified sweet wine and will include *vino liquoroso* on the label. I happen to like the cheap stuff, especially for cooking or dunking, but it's worth seeking out the true aged *vin santo*, either for yourself or as a gift for someone special. Some of the best *vin santo* is made by Avignonese, Isole e Olena, and Badia a Coltibuono.

Vino Sfuso

When I lived in Venice many years ago, I loved the little *vino sfuso* bottegas. These were places with big barrels where you could go with a glass or plastic bottle and have it filled with decent red or white wine, or even Prosecco on tap, for next to nothing—and the wine was actually pretty good.

In the past couple of years, there has been an explosion of *vino sfuso* outposts in Florence. Some offer a large range of reds and whites, plus a rosé and extra virgin olive oil. Others have just a few from which to choose. In either case, it's a very inexpensive way to buy wine, usually about three euros per bottle. You can bring your own bottle, or you can buy one there, which is then corked for you. The wine itself ranges from poor to decent to pretty darn good. *Sfuso* by definition will never be a fine DOC wine, because the bottling process is part of the DOC protocol, but it may be an IGT, at best, or more often a table wine that specifies its provenance and grape makeup. Most proprietors are happy to let you can taste the wines before you buy, and many will deliver cases to your home, which is an added bonus. Here are a few of the places close to the center, though there are many more.

La Buca del Vino
Via Romana 129r, 055/233-5021
Open Monday through Saturday, 10 AM to 1 PM and 5 PM to 8 PM
Map B7

Il Bacco Nudo
Via de' Macci, 59-61r, 055/243-298
Open Monday through Saturday, 9 AM to 1 PM and 4 PM to 8 PM
Map I4

Enoteca Vitae
Borgo La Croce 75r, 055/246-6503
Open daily 9 AM to 1 PM and 4 PM to 8:30 PM
Map H5

Grabbing a snack at All'Antico Vinaio.

Grappa

Grappa, the remarkably strong after-dinner brandy made from the skins and seeds (pomace) of wine grapes left over in the fermenting tanks, was once associated primarily with the north, particularly the Veneto, where the town of Bassano del Grappa is as famous for this heady spirit as it is for its covered bridge designed by Andrea Palladio. But as with almost every other possible area of wine and wine-related production, Tuscan producers have made serious inroads. You'll now see the elegantly designed bottles containing pure, clear grappa from Brunello, Chianti, Vernaccia, and almost every other type of Tuscan wine. Look for such producers as Antinori, Frescobaldi, Ornellaia, Il Poggiolo of Carmignano, and San Giorgio of Montalcino.

One of the friendly waiters at Osteria de' Benci.

3

DUOMO AND
AROUND

It's difficult to conceive of a small area anywhere in the world as packed with artistic treasures as the center of Florence. In terms of high Renaissance art and architecture, there is no parallel. No wonder so many people crowd these narrow streets all year long. Luckily, the center of Florence also offers several stops for delicious food and drink, whether a snack or a full meal. After all, you can only look at so many churches and paintings before you hunger for a cappuccino and a *dolce*, or a perfectly put together *panino*. This chapter covers the area comprising the Duomo, the Palazzo Vecchio, and the Uffizzi, as well as Piazza della Repubblica and the surrounding area.

RESTAURANTS AND TRATTORIAS

Alle Murate
Via del Proconsolo 16r, 055/240-618
Open Tuesday through Sunday 8 PM to 11 PM
€€€€
Map F4

The owners of Alle Murate spent a year and untold euros refurbishing this historic palazzo as the site of their flagship restaurant (the same family owns Osteria del Caffè Italiano). In the process, they uncovered a foundation that dates to Roman times, and original frescoes from the fourteenth century. Only in Italy. (The frescoes are so rare and important that they have their own audio guide and can be visited separately, by appointment, when the restaurant is closed.)

The restaurant is on three levels. On the top, an intimate candlelit room of linen-topped tables sits near the priceless frescoes. The scene on the ground floor is more sleek and contemporary, with a fountain in front of the partly open kitchen. Downstairs, the ambience is somewhat cavelike—as if you're dining in an archeological site, but with elegant linens and service—and the Plexiglas floor, which allows you to marvel at the nearly two-thousand-year-old foundation, is also a little dizzying.

The food is elegant and satisfying without being particularly over-whelming. As you can imagine, this is one restaurant where the food—no matter how wonderful—takes a backseat to the ambience. Some dishes, such as a chickpea soup garnished with shrimp and a tender filet mignon, can be excellent, however, while others can too often fall short. A tasting menu should be an opportunity for any chef to show off the best he or she's got, but here the menu, while good, is not memorable. Yet, for anyone looking for an elegant, gracious, and unique dining experience, this place is certain to please.

Osteria de' Benci

Via dei Benci 13r, 055/234-4923
Open daily 1 PM to 3 PM and 8 PM to 11 PM; closed two weeks in August
€€
Map F6

Reading the long, esoteric menu at Osteria de' Benci is like trying to enter into the brain of a sometimes lucid, sometimes mad chef—capricious, hard to fathom, but with moments of brilliance along with the incomprehensible. I recommend sticking to the more traditional Tuscan fare and forgiving the chef his trespasses as he forgives those who ask him to cook the *bistecca* well-done.

The signature dish—popular with many diners—is the *spaghetti dell'ubriacone* (drunken spaghetti), pasta boiled in wine so that it turns a bright burgundy and then tossed with garlic, olive oil, red pepper flakes, and parsley. The most successful primi are simple pastas: *spaghetti alla carbonara*, or a summery *tagliolini* with cherry tomatoes and grated Parmesan. Other selections change monthly to reflect the seasons, but there is always a focus on meat. You won't be disappointed with their *bistecca* or *tagliata* with arugula and Parmesan. The restaurant also offers a fair number of rabbit, chicken, and pork dishes, often roasted or grilled and served with small sides. Some desserts are made in-house, but I recommend you try those brought in from Dolce & Dolcezze (see page 86), including the raspberry tart and chocolate tart.

In winter, Benci is a cozy outpost with art-covered walls, brick-vaulted ceiling, and a big basement room for overflow. In summer, one entire wall opens onto the street, and the shrub-enclosed patio outside bustles until the wee hours. The restaurant's young owner and friendly, energetic staff keep things hopping, if not always efficient.

Cantinetta Antinori

Palazzo Antinori, Piazza Antinori 3, 055/292-234
Open Monday through Friday 12:30 PM to 3:30 PM and 7:30 PM to 10:30 PM;
closed most of August and Christmas week

€€€
Map D4

Cantinetta Antinori is a quiet and elegant oasis in the center of Florence's designer shopping district, both physically and spiritually near Ferragamo and Armani but owned by Tuscany's first family of wine. Double glass doors keep out the extremes of weather; crisp white tablecloths, fine stemware, and trained waitstaff make this place as popular with upscale travelers as with the local elite.

The *cantinetta* is both a showcase for the Antinori family's roster of wines and a font of traditional Tuscan cooking taken seriously. *Ribollita* and *panzanella* (served in winter and summer, respectively) are made according to stringent traditional recipes and with the freshest ingredients, including oil culled from Antinori properties. Other antipasti and primi might include simple dishes like prosciutto and melon or fresh porcini bathed in olive oil. For secondi, you can choose lighter fare, such as a seafood and white bean salad, or something as meaty as classic osso buco. Daily specials, where the chef typically gets a little more creative, might include an original—and excellent—swordfish fillet sandwiched between thin pieces of puff pastry, or a refreshing cold soup made from zucchini and mint. The wine list—all from the various Antinori estates—includes everyday fare like Santa Cristina on up to Tignanello, with plenty of drinkable whites and reds in between. The price of a meal here is on the high end for *ribollita* but not unfathomable—about what you'd expect to pay for dining in style in one of central Florence's most beautiful Renaissance palazzi.

Coquinarius

Via dell'Oche 15r, 055/230-2153
Open daily 9 AM to midnight; closed August
€€
Map F4

Coquinarius is a great combination of wine bar, restaurant, and stop for a light bite at odd hours. It also has the distinction of being about ten paces away from the Duomo, on a small side street. The evocative space, with its high ceilings and brick walls, is made comfortable and pleasant with modern track lighting, distressed furniture, and French and Italian posters from the 1920s and 1930s. A handful of white and red wines are available by the glass at reasonable prices, and there is a much longer list of bottles. The menu is distinguished by its popular *insalatone*—big salads with interesting combinations of ingredients. The kitchen also turns out simple but excellent pastas and other hot primi, including a great potato gnocchi with Gorgonzola sauce. Prices are reasonable and service is friendly, though it can be slow at peak times.

Frescobaldi Ristorante & Wine Bar

Via dei Magazzini 2–4r, 055/284-724
**Open Monday through Saturday noon to 3:30 PM and 7 PM to 10:30 PM; closed
   Monday lunch**
€€€
Map F5

Not to be outdone by the Antinori family and their *cantinetta* (page 45),
one of the other primary aristocratic Tuscan winemaking families, the
Frescobaldis, opened their own restaurant and wine bar a few years ago,
right in the center of town, next to the Palazzo Vecchio. This is a major
undertaking, a sprawling, multiroom space with cool stone floors and
walls painted in burnt ochre to look like draperies. Tables are covered
with white cloths and topped with candles. The staff and menu are multilingual.

The simple yet appealing menu features a number of appealing fresh
pasta dishes, as well as spaghetti *caccio e pepe*, a Roman specialty that
combines Pecorino Romano cheese and cracked black peppercorns.
Secondi include such Tuscan standards as roasted pork with herbs and
rabbit stuffed with prunes.

Not surprisingly, the restaurant is a showcase for the Frescobaldi
wines and olive oils. The wine list is made up entirely of Frescobaldi offerings, including wines from their holdings in Chile and from
their partners, such as Mondavi in California. Because Frescobaldi makes
so many wines, the choices don't come across as limited. You can order
bottles from Luce and Lucente (including older vintages), Ornellaia,
Castelgiocondo, and several others. Also part of the operation is Fres-
cobaldini, a cute, casual wine bar with a wooden counter and a few stools
where you can stop for a glass of wine and a snack. The entrance is on Via
della Condotta.

All'Antico Vinaio

Via dei Neri 65r, 055/238-2723

Open daily 9 AM to 3 PM and 5 PM to 7 PM; closed Sunday afternoons and Monday mornings; closed August

Map F5

Around noon and before dinner every evening, this little wine bar overflows onto the street with happy snackers. It's a good choice for a light bite or glass of Chianti, especially if you don't mind standing, as the few bar stools go fast. The draws are great-looking crostini topped with artichoke, tomato, and liver pâté; attractive platters of cooked pasta; and little sandwiches, all meant to be downed quickly with an inexpensive glass of wine.

Cantinetta dei Verrazzano

Via dei Tavolini 18–20r, 055/268-590

Open Monday through Saturday 8 AM to 9 PM (lunch served 12:30 PM to 2:30 PM); closed two weeks in August

Map E4

The Cantinetta is a kind of small-scale gourmet food hall. The bakery at the front sells outstanding breads, cookies, and cakes, such as *torta della nonna* and a chocolate-semolina concoction. Beyond the baked goods, you'll find a marble-topped bar serving top-quality Piansa coffee. Stop here in the morning for a cappuccino and pastry; you won't even have to pay extra to sit at one of the few tables. At lunch, squeeze into the boxcar-sized room next-door for fantastic focaccia sandwiches straight from the wood-fired oven, tasting plates of Cinta Senese *salumi* (see page 26), cheeses paired with spicy *mostarda*, and other treats.

The place has plenty of charm, with marble-topped tables and ornate wooden cabinets showing off bottles of Verrazzano wine (also for sale here). In all, this is a great spot to have lunch before visiting the Duomo or Palazzo Vecchio. If the wait for one of the handful of tables looks long, you can always order a sandwich and a drink and eat while sitting on the

Tripe Sellers: The Offal Truth

The freewheeling tripe sellers who hawk their hot sandwiches from little mobile carts are a Florentine tradition, and for a long time these sandwiches were the favorite quick lunch of the working class. Today the *trippai* are an endangered species, but you can still find a few die-hard vendors offering both tripe and *lampredotto* (from the fourth stomach; tripe is from the first), their carts usually surrounded by a crowd of delighted eaters—everyone from art students to carpenters to university professors. Choose from tripe *paniabili*, served on a round roll with *salsa verde* (green sauce), or a *fiorentina* with tomato sauce and Parmesan. You'll find some of the best *trippai* outside the Porta Romana, next to the south entrance of Boboli Gardens; at the corner of Via dei Macci and Borgo la Croce, right near the Sant'Ambrogio market; and in Piazza dei Cimatori, in front of the American Express office.

long wooden bench or leaning against the bar. The prices here are a bit high, but the appeal of the setting, the quality of the food, and the location all justify the cost.

Forno Sartoni
Via dei Cerchi 34r, 055/212-570
Open Monday through Saturday 7:45 AM to 8 PM; closed part of August
Map E5

Forno Sartoni serves several purposes: it is a good bakery, selling baguettes, rounds, and all kinds of breads with and without salt; it's a place to pick up fresh sweets like *papatacci*, a flat breakfast roll filled with raisins; and it is a nice spot for a snack when you are in the center of town. The pizzas—Margherita, marinara, onion, and potato—are all served by the slice and priced by weight. The sandwiches, usually on focaccia, are also excellent; I've enjoyed the tuna, the roasted eggplant, and several others. This place is often crowded, and you either have to get your food to go or lean against a railing along the wall—not the most comfortable way to enjoy lunch, but very quick and easy.

I Fratellini
Via dei Cimatori 38r, 055/239-6096
Open daily 8 AM to 7 PM (closed Sunday in winter); closed August
Map E5

Along with Forno Sartoni, Fratellini is a lifesaver for anyone who's hungry and in a hurry in the center of town. For years, this little stall has been doling out small, perfectly proportioned sandwiches of pecorino and arugula, goat cheese and wild boar salami, mozzarella and tomato, and anchovies and butter, all accompanied by gulp-sized glasses of good wine or soda. Try the sun-dried tomato sandwich with goat cheese, or the pecorino and arugula with truffle oil. All the sandwiches are served on delicious warm rosette rolls. You eat standing on the street leaning against the wall or crouching on the sidewalk, so if you're tired from walking around all day, this isn't your best option.

GustaVino

Via della Condotta 37r, 055/239-9806
Open Monday through Saturday 6 PM to 11 PM; closed one week in August
Map E5

This is one of the newfangled wine bars—all polished glass and stainless steel—that has recently conquered Florence. In the early evening, you can belly up to the sleek bar for a glass of wine from an ample list and a taste of unusual appetizers, or you can come later in the evening for a whole meal. GustaVino is now owned by the same company that owns Lanciola wines.

The group has also opened up a new space next door called **La Canova di GustaVino**, which has a much more rustic Tuscan (Ruscan?) atmosphere. This is a great place to try a "Grande Degustazione" of local cheeses, salumi, wine, and/or olive oil.

Mariano

Via del Parione 19r, 055/214-067
Open Monday through Friday 8 AM to 3:30 PM and 5 PM to 7:30 PM, Saturday 8 AM to 3:30 PM; closed two weeks in August
Map D5

This little place is hidden on a narrow street between the Trinità and Carraia bridges. The only outdoor sign says simply *Alimentari*, but if you wander by around lunchtime, you can't help but hear the buzz emanating from within. Florentines flock here for their sandwiches, made to order, all for under three euros. It's not that easy to find tasty, freshly made sandwiches in Florence, and this is one of the few places where you can actually sit, or at least lean, and relax while you eat one. Choose from a long list that includes tuna, sausage, prosciutto, *lardo*, cheese, roast beef, and other simple fillings. The *bresaola* with arugula and cream cheese (Italians call it Philadelphia) is a surprisingly delicious combination. You can wash it down with a cold drink or an inexpensive glass of wine. (Mariano reopens in the evenings as a place to grab a glass of wine or an *aperitivo*, and opens early in the morning in case someone in the neighborhood needs a coffee.)

Procacci

Via Tornabuoni 64r, 055/211-656
Open Monday through Saturday 10:30 AM to 8:30 PM; closed August and
Christmas Day
Map D4

For a long time I ignored this little shop, squeezed between the Puccis and Guccis on Via Tornabuoni. (I usually try to avoid entering anything on this street, for fear I'll be put under fashion arrest.) Procacci, which is owned by the winemaking Antinori family, has specialized in truffles since 1885. Here you will find tempting little finger sandwiches filled with such luxury ingredients as smoked salmon and arugula, Brie and walnuts, and, of course, truffles—all for just a couple euros each. Procacci also carries a selection of gourmet goods, including its own line of truffle and mushroom spreads, cherry tomatoes in oil, and shallots in sweet-and-sour sauce. In the afternoon, when your feet are too sore to take another step, stop in for a snack, a glass of Antinori wine, and a dose of authentic old-world atmosphere.

WINE BARS AND WINE SHOPS

Alessi

Via dell'Oche 27–29r, 055/239-6987
Open Monday through Saturday 9 AM to 1 PM and 4 PM to 8 PM; closed August
Map E4

On its ground floor, Alessi is divided into a candy and gourmet sweet-shop on one side and a wine-tasting bar on the other. None of this seems particularly exciting until you descend the staircase to the wine cellar. Giorgio Alessi's wine selection is mind-boggling. You'll find bottle after bottle arranged by region; one room filled entirely with Tuscan wines is the size of most *enoteche*, and another equally big space is filled only with wines from Piedmont. This is also one of the few central *enoteche* to store the wines horizontally, in specially designed brick racks that resist heat and cold. In addition to the vast selection of contemporary wines,

Alessi has assembled a sort of wine museum, which is located in a dark, locked area and includes bottles from 1900 on. Upstairs you'll find spirits and dessert wines, including a vast choice of quality *vin santo*. Because of its reputation and central location, Alessi is popular with tourists and has a multilingual staff.

Gambi

Borgo SS. Apostoli 21–23r, 055/292-646
Open Monday through Friday 10 AM to 7 PM, Saturday 4 PM to 7 PM; closed
August
Map E5

The Gambi family has run this thriving wine shop since 1957. *La mamma* is still in attendance, but daughter Elena, with a sommelier degree and several languages under her belt, has taken over much of the responsibility. Downstairs you'll find gourmet gift items like *limoncello*, *biscotti di Antonio Mattei* (see page 157), and balsamic vinegar from Modena, but the main action is upstairs in the wine room. The most expensive wines, including much-requested bottles of Tignanello and Le Pergole Torte, are kept in a glass case at the top of the stairs. Gambi stocks the major Chianti producers and also some interesting smaller estates, such as Terreno of Greve in Chianti, both a *riserva* and Chianti Classico from Il Tarroco, and a Sangiovese-Cabernet mix from Podere San Luigi. It carries a wide selection of wines from Piedmont and other Italian regions, and an impressive stock of white wines, often an afterthought in wine shops. Among the whites, you'll find a Verncaccia di San Gimignano from Pernizzi, with cool modern label design, and Batar, a white made by Querciabella, better known for its Chiantis. (Gambi has another location outside the Porta Romana at Via Senese 21r, 055/222-525.)

Chiaroscuro

Via del Corso 36r, 055/214-247
Open Monday through Friday 8 AM to 8:30 PM, Saturday and Sunday 8 AM to
9:30 PM; closed Sunday in summer
Map E4

Chiaroscuro is a pleasant place to take shelter from the busy Corso shopping street. You can either stand at the bar, or sit in the bistrolike back room outfitted with cane chairs and a few little tables, and sip a *nocciolina*, a coffee, cream, and hazelnut concoction served in little glass cups. I have a lifelong grudge against flavored coffee, but I make an exception for the *nocciolina* and the *bicchierina*, an equally divine mix of coffee, chocolate, and cream. You can also buy roasted coffee beans from all over the world. At lunchtime, you might satisfy your appetite with a light Niçoise salad, a heaping plate of pasta, or a salad from the glass case in front. In the evening, Chiaroscuro also hosts a popular aperitivo hour, featuring a different international theme (sushi, Middle Eastern food) almost every night.

Donnini

Piazza della Repubblica 15r, 055/213-694
Open Thursday through Tuesday 7 AM to 1 AM; closed part of August
Map E4

Donnini is literally dwarfed by the other cafés in this grand nineteenth-century piazza, so I was glad when a Florentine friend first directed me here to try the *caffè macchiato* (served in a little glass cup), one of the best in the city. Donnini is now under new ownership and is a little bit more pretentious and tourist oriented than it once was, but the coffee is still very good, and at lunchtime, you can still try one of its inexpensive and tasty hot pastas, which emerge from the kitchen in big serving dishes. (There is usually room to perch on a stool or lean at the bar, but don't come here if you really want to sit down and relax.)

Gilli

Piazza della Repubblica 36–39r, 055/213-896
Open Wednesday through Monday 7:30 AM to 10 PM; closed August
Map E4

Part of Piazza della Repubblica's troika of elegant, Viennese-style cafés, which also includes Paszkowski and Giubbe Rosse (once the hangout of Florence's poets and artists), Gilli is known for both its chocolates and its *aperitivi*, and like the others, it's a good central stop for a coffee and brioche or *bombolone* (doughnut). The drinking starts early, so don't be surprised to see fur-clad women and old men in hats lined up against the wood-and-mirror art nouveau bar at noon on a weekday, sipping Prosecco and partaking of the impressive spread of snacks. A glass case next to the cash register displays a beautiful array of chocolates, both light and dark.

Caffè Italiano

Via della Condotta 56r, 055/291-082
Open Monday through Saturday 8 AM to 8 PM (daily in June and July); closed August
Map E5

This elegant belle epoque–style café with dark wood paneling, crystal chandeliers, and wrought-iron chairs is another welcome spot in the center of town: an excellent place to duck in for a morning hot chocolate while you browse the various international newspapers hanging on hooks. There is also a cozy upstairs room, where you can order coffee and pastries, or a light lunch of soup or pasta.

Migone

Via dei Calzaiuoli 85–87r, 055/214-004
Open Tuesday through Saturday 9 AM to 7:30 PM; closed Christmas Day
Map E4

Next to the expensive leather goods and high-fashion *botteghe* on Via dei Calzaiuoli, Migone is a gift boutique of sweets. You can stock up on locally made biscotti, all manner of candy kitsch such as chocolates shaped like the Duomo and the Baptistry, colorful Sicilian marzipan fruits, and different flavors of *torrone* (nougat).

Paszkowski

Piazza della Repubblica 31–35r, 055/210-236
Open Tuesday through Sunday 7:30 AM to 1 AM
Map E4

Owned by the same family as Gilli next-door, Paszkowski has been serving Florence's best dressed since 1846. The buttoned-up ambience is definitely snooty, but it's worth putting up with to discover Gilli's little tarts: yogurt tarts with berries, custard tarts with chocolate, orange- or lime-custard tarts with little pieces of fruit on top, all lined up like a beauty pageant under glass. People come on weekends and fill up elegant boxes to bring to a party or a family lunch. On top of the counter, you'll see thick bars of *nocciolato* (chocolate hazelnut) prettily wrapped in cellophane with the house label. The little chocolate cookies, meringue kisses, and *babas* floating in a big bowl of rum are all equally tempting. Paszkowski has a large indoor room for eating, and plenty of space outside, but I wouldn't recommend either if you're on a budget.

Rivoire

Piazza della Signoria 5r, 055/214-412

Open Tuesday through Saturday 8 AM to 12:30 AM in summer, 8 AM to 9 PM in winter; closed Christmas Day

Map E5

It may be touristy and straight out of a postcard, but from this prime spot on Piazza Signoria, you can indulge in Rivoire's famous hot chocolate with whipped cream (*cioccolata calda con panna*) or cappuccino right in view of the Palazzo Vecchio and the Uffizi. You can also do as the locals do and take your *cioccolata* while standing at the counter for a lot less money. The chocolate is thick, dark, and rich, and the light whipped cream balances out some of the heaviness. It's a perfect pick-me-up on a gloomy or rainy day. Rivoire also sells its own brand of packaged chocolates (many filled with liqueur) and makes an excellent *torta della nonna* to enjoy while people-watching and gazing at the copy of *David* in front of the Palazzo Vecchio.

Robiglio

Via dei Servi 112r, 055/214-501

Open Monday through Saturday 7:30 AM to 7:30 PM, Saturday 7:30 AM to 2 PM in summer; closed August and New Year's Day

Map F3

Via dei Tosinghi 11r, 055/215-013

Open Monday through Saturday 8 AM to 8 PM; closed August and New Year's Day

Map E4

The original location of Robiglio on Via dei Servi is an incredibly popular place for coffee and delicious pastry. The *bariste* are constantly singing, and there's a lot of loud and lively chatter in the packed space around the bar. Among the specialties are *tortine della nonna* and *nonno* (with chocolate), lemon-custard tartlets, and brioches. The savories (small *panini* and slices of rustic vegetable tarts) are also good, and crowds stand around eating them at lunch. The shop sells row after row of small chocolate candies, as well as a variety of European packaged brands. Here's a tip for pastry success: the top shelf holds whatever just came out of the oven.

If you're shopping in the city center, stop in at the Via dei Tosinghi location, between Via dei Calzaiuoli and Piazza della Repubblica. The always-festive window displays show off the good-looking cakes and tortes inside. Robiglio also serves an excellent cappuccino and *caffè macchiato*.

The welcoming staff at Robiglio.

Chocolate Valley

One of the latest trends in Tuscan gastronomy is high-quality artisanal chocolates. The critical mass of some of the biggest names in Italian chocolate, including **Catinari** in the small town of Agliana, near Pisa; **Paul De Bondt** of Pisa; **Slitti** (pronounced zlee-tee) in the spa town of Monsummano Terme; and **Amadei** in Pontedera, near Pistoia, has led the food and wine magazine **Gambero Rosso** to dub the northeast corner of Tuscany "Chocolate Valley." You can find chocolates from Slitti and Paul De Bondt at **Hemingway** (see page 134), and from Amadei at **Chiaroscuro** (see page 55), **Procacci** (see page 53), and **Gambi** (see page 54), among other places.

GELATO

Carrozza
Piazza del Pesce 3–5, 055/239-6810
Open Thursday through Tuesday 11 AM to 1 AM
Map E5

Before I moved to Florence, people who had lived here told me to make sure to go to "the gelateria near the Ponte Vecchio." The only problem was that there were at least three gelaterias on each side of the bridge. But soon I followed my nose—and the line of people—and figured out they were talking about Carrozza, the best gelato in the immediate vicinity. The shop makes an excellent chocolate flavor, and the *pistacchio*, *nocciola* (hazelnut), and yogurt are all creamy treats. The fruit flavors are deep and colorful, including a refreshing lemon and a dark and tempting *mirtillo* (blueberry).

Friendly server at Carrozza.

Grom

Via delle Oche 24r, 055/216-158
Open daily 10:30 AM to 12 AM
Map E4

Grom may not be homegrown—this expanding chain hails from Turin—but it has quickly been acknowledged as one of the best gelaterias in town, by visitors and locals alike. On a quiet street just around the corner from the Duomo, Grom offers creamy, rich gelato made from the finest Italian ingredients. The atmosphere is rather hushed and serious, and the gelato is hidden under metal tops, much like the famous Gelateria San Crispino in Rome, instead of displayed in a gigantic airy, pastel wave, the more typical style in Florence. What's hiding in those metal tubs? Some of the best chocolate, cream, and nut flavors this side of the Arno. Not surprisingly, the *gianduja*, a specialty of Turin, is one of the standouts, as are the pistachio and the brightly delicious fruit sorbets. If you are staying in the area, you'll probably want to come here more than once to make sure you don't miss anything important.

Bartolini

Via dei Servi 30r, 055/211-895
Open Monday through Saturday 9 AM to 1 PM and 3:30 PM to 7:30 PM; closed
Monday morning in winter and Saturday afternoon in summer; closed
most of August
Map F3

The service can be frustrating, but Bartolini is probably the best place in Florence to buy straightforward kitchen goods (as opposed to gifts). On one end of the store are nicely displayed shelves of fancy wares, including Wedgwood and Richard Ginori china, gleaming espresso machines, Riedel wineglasses, copper pots, and a whole line of goods by Alessi. On the other end are the practical cooking items, such as inexpensive stainless-steel pots with heavy bottoms, Wüsthof knives, and every conceivable gadget for making Italian food: pasta machines and cutters, pie rollers, olive-oil taps, and more sizes, shapes, and styles of stove-top coffeemakers than I've ever seen. Check out the *chitarra*, an extraordinary little device that looks like a musical instrument but is actually used for cutting fresh pasta into long, squared-off strands. At least one English-speaking staff member is usually on hand to answer questions.

Coin Casa

Via dei Calzaioli 56r (basement of Coin department store), 055/280-531
Open Monday through Saturday 9:30 AM to 8 PM, Sunday 11 AM to 8 PM
Map E5

The large basement of this upscale department store harbors some excellent—and affordable—goods for both the kitchen and dining room. Don't come here if you are looking for distinctively Italian or Tuscan wares to bring home. Instead, this is where locals stock up on colorful woven place mats, well-made cotton tablecloths, traditional and Japanese-influenced ceramics, and accessories like candles and cloth napkins. You can also buy kitchen utensils, pots, pans, mitts, and a big array of other basic necessities, all well displayed.

Pegna

Via dello Studio 8, 055/282-701

Open Monday through Saturday 9 AM to 1 PM and 4 PM to 8 PM in winter, daily 9 AM to 1 PM and 3:30 PM to 5:30 PM in summer

Map F4

In Italy, you often find little stores that sell the strangest combinations of items: pet food and toilet paper, tobacco and salt, baby toys and pharmaceuticals, to name just a few. Pegna takes this quirky tradition to new heights. The front section resembles a posh drugstore, with ordinary household products, like tissues and toothpaste. But beyond it, the good stuff begins. First you come to the spice counter, where you can pick up shelled pistachios, fennel seeds, and other baking and cooking ingredients. Next is the chocolate and sweets section, filled with Lindt and Perugina, as well as lots of gifty items. Then you stumble on the liquors, with Champagne, cognac, organic local wines, and the like. Turn the corner and you'll find an array of gourmet dried pastas, estate-bottled oils, and aged balsamic vinegars, along with specialty goods like jarred stuffed peppers. A tiny deli offers gorgeous *salumi,* some ready-made sauces, imported Cheddar and Stilton cheeses, and beautiful—and expensive—Norwegian smoked salmon.

Richard Ginori

Via Rondinelli 17r, 055/210-041

Open Monday through Friday 10 AM to 7 PM, Saturday 9 AM to 1 PM; closed Saturday and Monday in winter

Map D4

Richard Ginori makes some of the most beautiful bone china and hand-painted porcelain in the world. This fancy showroom displays china, porcelain, stunning silver trays and serving pieces, and some vases and larger pieces that have "wedding gift" written all over them. The prices may be lower here than in the United States and elsewhere (depending on the exchange rate), but remember to factor in the price of shipping your purchases home. (Come dressed to impress if you want any attention from the jaded saleswomen.) The showroom for the Richard Ginori kitchen and bath collection is further out of town in Sesto Fiorentino (Viale Giulio Cesare 21, tel. 055/420-491; fax 055/420-4934); call for an appointment.

Sbigoli

Via Sant'Egidio 4r, 055/247-9713
Open Monday through Saturday 9:00 AM to 1 PM and 3 PM to 7:30 PM
Map G4

I've come here often to buy wedding presents for friends when I want something that exudes true Italian-ness. Sbigoli sells lovely pieces, both hand-painted ceramics typical of Deruta, in Umbria, and the studio's own largely floral designs. You can choose from mugs and teacups, large and small serving bowls and platters, and decorative as well as everyday plates. The owners speak English, accept credit cards, and are adept at packing and shipping.

Tassini

Borgo SS. Apostoli 24r, 055/282-696
Open Monday through Saturday 8:30 AM to 2:30 PM and 4:30 PM to 7:30 PM;
closed most of August
Map D5

Despite its touristy trappings (the color brochure is in Italian, English, and Japanese), this little *alimentari* on a side street near the Ponte Vecchio is worth a stop for wine and certain gourmet foods. It sells a fine assortment of Italian wines from Tuscany, Piedmont, and other areas, including names like Gaja, Barbi, and Castello di Ama, and stocks several shelves with an impressive array of jams, *mostarde*, honeys, and expensive concoctions made with white and black truffles. You'll also find a small sampling of estate-bottled olive oils, dried pastas in funny shapes and colors, and biscotti from Antonio Mattei of Prato (see page 157).

Libreria Edison

Piazza della Repubblica 27r, 055/213-110
Open Monday through Saturday 9 AM to 12 AM, Sunday 10 AM to 12 AM
Map E4

With its four floors of books, a small café with tables and chairs for reading, and American-style open-all-hours schedule, Edison is a true respite in central Florence. It is often the only place to hang out on a rainy Sunday or to find air-conditioned solace on an August afternoon. It stocks a fair number of English-language cookbooks and food-related guidebooks on the ground floor near the cash registers, including huge stacks of *Gambero Rosso*'s wine guides and other favorites. The third floor houses a decent Italian-language cookbook and food history section, in addition to English-language novels and recent nonfiction releases.

Feltrinelli International

Via Cavour 12r, 055/292-196
Open Monday through Saturday 9 AM to 7:30 PM
Map F3

All English speakers staying in Florence should be aware of Feltrinelli International for its great selections of English-language books. (It also stocks French, German, and, of course, Italian books.) Near the entrance, look for a stash of English-language guidebooks to the region and one whole shelf of cookbooks, including works by Marcella Hazan, Lorenza de' Medici, and Elizabeth David.

Paperback Exchange

Via delle Oche 4r, 055/293-460
Open Monday through Friday 9 AM to 7:30 PM, Saturday 10 AM to 7:30 PM
Map F4

Paperback Exchange, which sells books exclusively in English, recently relocated from Via Fiesolana to a bigger and nicer location in the city center. Many students in study-abroad programs buy their textbooks here, but you'll also find several shelves stocked with volumes on food and wine. The shop sells a lot of coffee-table books on Tuscany and Florence, as well as wine guides and cookbooks, including titles by Benedetta Vitali of Zibibbo (see page 151) and Jamie Oliver. It even carries books on sushi and *The Joy of Cooking*, for those tired of Italian fare. The entire staff is English speaking and will help you find or order whatever you are looking for.

One of the busy produce stands at the Sant'Ambrogio market.

4
SANTA CROCE

Santa Croce is the city's spectacular fourteenth-century Franciscan church, famous for housing the tombs of a trio of celebrated Florentines, Michelangelo, Machiavelli, and Galileo, and for its frescoes by Giotto, Cimabue, and others. Each June, the large, bustling piazza in front of the church serves as the site of the *calcio storico*, a rough-and-tumble "historical soccer" match played by representatives from the city's four oldest quarters. And in December, the entire piazza is taken over by a northern European–style Christmas market, featuring bratwurst, beer, and lots of colorful toys and gifts.

The area around Santa Croce lies to the east of the Uffizi and the Duomo, toward the old medieval walls of the eastern edge of the city (now largely gone, but traced by the multilane *viali* that pass through Piazza Beccaria). For the most part, the neighborhood has maintained its medieval and Renaissance character, with narrow streets, imposing palace facades, and vibrant stores and markets. For the sake of this book, I am calling anything in this eastern quadrant Santa Croce, including the essential Mercato di Sant'Ambrogio and the eateries that surround it, and the excellent sweetshops and lunch spots around Piazza Beccaria. Santa Croce is very much part of central Florence and is home to some of the city's best restaurants and a surprisingly high number of first-rate gelaterias.

Trattoria Baldovino

Via San Giuseppe 22r (off Piazza Santa Croce), 055/241-773
Open daily 11:30 PM to 2:30 PM and 7 PM to 11:30 PM
€€
Map G5

Noisy, popular Baldovino is the creation of Scottish restaurateur David Gardner, who is also responsible for the Baldovino wine bar next-door (see page 82) and Beccofino (see page 114) across the Arno. The menu is broad enough to please everyone in a group (in fact, this is one of the best places in the city to come with picky eaters), with a wine list to match. Start with antipasti of crostini and prosciutto, or with something more unusual, like swordfish carpaccio with arugula and radicchio. From there, you can pick and choose from various types of focaccia, which are like giant no-cheese pizzas; big salads; and a wide choice of primi and secondi. The pizzas here are cooked in a wood-fired oven—try the Baldovino, with prosciutto, arugula, and Parmesan, or the *crudaiola*, with fresh ricotta and chopped tomatoes. The pastas and gnocchi are good and hearty, with black truffles or porcini and rabbit *ragù* in winter, and *spaghetti alla carbonara* or *maltagliati* with zucchini flowers in summer. For a secondo, you might try the *tagliata* (sliced steak) or saltimbocca. If you still have room, finish off with a slice of one of the superb house-made cakes. The wine list offers plenty of choices, mainly Tuscan but also from other regions. This is also an excellent place to try some unusual dessert wines by the glass.

The restaurant is usually crowded (often with English-speaking tourists), so diners are sometimes herded through the meal without the customary Italian table-lingering time. And the harried staff can seem so overworked that it's no surprise when service is slow or slapdash. The vestibule-like front room has been improved, but I still prefer to sit in the main dining room, with its open kitchen, country French–style wooden tables and chairs, and colorful paintings.

Boccadama

Piazza Santa Croce 25–26r, 055/243-640
Open daily 8:30 AM to midnight; closed Monday evening in winter
€€
Map G5

I was wary of Boccadama at first, because of its touristy location, right in busy Piazza Santa Croce. But in fact, this place is the real thing: an exceedingly pleasant casual restaurant and wine bar with a small menu of modestly unusual takes on Tuscan cuisine. And it offers a good opportunity to match excellent Italian wines by the glass with various flavors from the adept kitchen.

Start your meal with white wine—a Tuscan Chardonnay or a Friulian Sauvignon Blanc—and French cheeses with white wine confiture, salty mixed Tuscan *salumi*, and thinly sliced *lardo di Colonnata* on toasts. The kitchen also makes an excellent bruschetta with tomato and basil. For the main course, you might move to a red wine, such as a Tuscan IGT blend of Cabernet Sauvignon with Cabernet Franc, or Sangiovese blended with Merlot, both of which go well with the roast lamb or the potato ravioli topped with wild boar *ragù*. For lighter fare, try the *zuppa di ceci* (chickpea soup), or *trenette* (long, narrow flat pasta) with pesto. For dessert, the incredibly dense *torta al cioccolato* pairs well with some of the sharper red dessert wines, or go with the classic pairing of biscotti and *vin santo*. In summer, the restaurant sets up a wooden platform right in the piazza for outdoor seating.

Osteria del Caffè Italiano

Via Isola delle Stinche 11–13r, 055/289-368
Open Tuesday through Sunday 12:30 PM to 3 PM and 5:30 PM to 11 PM
€€
Map F5

Osteria del Caffè Italiano has a lot going for it. The spacious restaurant is housed in a beautiful old building on a curving street just around the corner from Piazza Santa Croce. The interior, with its high ceilings, old apothecary's cabinets on one wall, and huge prosciutto slicer right at the entrance, has the kind of authentic yet elegant ambience that people are looking for on a trip to Florence. On weekdays, the kitchen serves an inexpensive light lunch of soups and salads; at night (and weekend days) the dining room (and patio in summer) is dressed up with white linen tablecloths and candlelight. The food is traditional Tuscan. You're wise to order anything cooked in the wood-fired oven, especially the *arista* (roasted pork) wrapped in pancetta and sage. Simple veal and lamb chops and vegetable side dishes are also served, and the wine list is extensive. Desserts here are very good, including the house-made tarts of fruit or chocolate. Or, you can opt for a gelato from Vivoli (see page 88) just down the street. The osteria also operates a tiny, excellent pizzeria next-door (see page 79) that's well worth a visit.

Ristorante Cibreo

Via del Verrocchio 8r, 055/234-1100
Open Tuesday through Saturday 1 PM to 2:30 PM and 7 PM to 11 PM; closed
August
€€€€
Map H4

Cibreo's fame and fortune can be measured in part by its international clientele: diners come from far and wide to sample chef-owner Fabio Picchi's legendary fare. In 1979, Picchi and Benedetta Vitali (see pages 76, 151) decided to open a restaurant that was at once innovative and traditionally Tuscan, dedicated to bringing back the long-forgotten peasant cooking of the region. Their efforts have reinvigorated Florentine and Tuscan cooking during the past decades.

Picchi is known for his eccentricities, which shine through in the unusual dining experience. Large groups are seated at their own tables, but solo diners and couples share large round tables, which can be fun or a little awkward. Possibly the best part of dinner is the assortment of antipasti served alongside a glass of fruity white wine. Local pecorino and walnuts come bathed in a strong, garlicky olive oil; also full of garlic and spice is the house's signature tomato parfait, which tastes like a gazpacho mousse. For a primo, you can choose from among Tuscan soups or stews made with *farro*, polenta, *cavolo nero*, or other rustic ingredients. Take note, however, that Cibreo, perhaps alone in the entire Italian peninsula, serves *no pasta*.

When it comes to secondi, you can almost picture the devilish Picchi, with his wizardlike gray beard, giggling with glee as he imagines what tricks he can pull on unsuspecting tourists; he would like to to challenge and possibly even shock them out of culinary complacence. Whereas any American chef knows he or she must stack the main-course deck with steaks and chicken dishes because that's what people want, Picchi will not be limited by mob rule. The secondi menu is made up almost entirely of preparations rarely found on an American menu: calves' brains, pig's trotters . . . it begins to sound a bit like the witches' brew from *Macbeth*. The most "normal" dishes on the menu might be something like sea bass baked in tomato sauce or roasted pigeon with sweet-and-sour *mostarda*—itself an haute-Tuscan classic.

Trattoria Cibreo (also called Cibreino) ✳

Via dei Macci 122r, 055/234-1100 (no reservations)
Open Tuesday through Saturday 1 PM to 2:30 PM and 7 PM to 11 PM; closed August
€€
Map H4

As the more casual counterpart to the famous Ristorante Cibreo (see opposite), this small trattoria is a fun and delicious experience. The two Cibreos share a kitchen and many menu items, so you can taste the same innovative takes on traditional Tuscan dishes, but in a relaxed atmosphere and at a fraction of the price. Some of the standard dishes include the tomato parfait antipasto and some simple primi like *infarinata* with *cavolo nero*, a grainy yet creamy soup with black cabbage, and homemade *passatelli* noodles floating in meat broth. The secondi are even better, if more challenging: although the stuffed chicken neck sounds unappetizing, it is actually a delicious cold chicken mousse, sliced and served with a lemony homemade mayonnaise. It does, however, arrive with the bird's head (albeit roasted) on the plate. A few fish dishes are served every night, often something with *baccalà* (salt cod) or *stoccafisso* (unsalted dried cod). The wine list has several affordable options. Try to leave room for dessert, especially anything with chocolate.

Considering how similar the food is at the restaurant and the trattoria, the difference in price is striking. I actually prefer the trattoria's understated décor of wooden tables and wall paneling, modern art, and dried chiles hanging from the ceiling. However, there is one big drawback: no reservations are taken, so on any given night you might end up waiting anywhere from ten minutes to an hour for a table. The trattoria is small, so it's a good idea to arrive either early, around 7 PM when the place opens, or late, after 10 PM.

La Pentola dell'Oro
Via di Mezzo 24–26r, 055/241-808
Open Monday through Saturday 1 PM to 3 PM and 7:30 PM to 10:30 PM
€
Map G4

Why is it that when an Italian restaurant is divided into two sections, one elegant and the other casual—in this case, a ristorante downstairs and an osteria upstairs—that I always favor the latter? Giuseppe Alessi and his crew create interesting menus for both floors, but I prefer the convivial feel—and the low prices—of the osteria to the hushed, windowless, and more expensive ristorante. The ambience upstairs is no-frills, with a few wooden tables topped with yellow paper placemats and a television tuned to news or sports.

The kitchen here is known for making some straightforward Tuscan dishes (good crostini with liver, pasta with porcini, roasted meats), but also for more experimental fare using herbs and spices rarely seen in Florence, such as horseradish, cardamom, and cumin. (One pasta dish with a kind of horseradish sauce is only for people with a fire hose or very cold glass of wine handy. It's like spaghetti with wasabi.) The pasta with spinach pesto is refreshing and light, while the fresh pasta with a pot roast–based *sugo* will warm you up on a cold winter night. Secondi are primarily stewed meats, and desserts are mostly a variation on the cream-on-a-spoon theme (*semifreddo, panna cotta*, crème caramel)—all quite satisfying, though I was surprised when my custard arrived on fire! The house white is unusually poor, so look to the wine list for a drinkable Chianti or other bottle. When you call to reserve, specify that you want to sit upstairs in the osteria, unless, of course, you're feeling fancy.

Enoteca Pinchiorri

Via Ghibellina 87, tel. 055/242-777; fax 055/244-983 (best to reserve at least two weeks in advance)

Open Tuesday and Wednesday 7:30 PM to 10 PM, Thursday through Saturday 12:30 PM to 2 PM and 7:30 PM to 10 PM; closed August and Christmas Day

€€€€

Map G5

First, money must be no object. Second, you should be excited by the kind of old-world elegance—sterling-silver water pitchers, Murano glass chandeliers, fine table linens, liveried waiters—that is a dying breed in this new world of sleek designer lighting and square plates. Third, you should be interested in wine. If all this sounds enticing, Enoteca Pinchiorri opens its Renaissance palazzo doors to you.

Pinchiorri is considered by some to be the best restaurant in Florence (it is the only restaurant in Florence with two Michelin stars) and is certainly the most expensive, costing almost $300 per person, before wine. Diners can choose between à la carte dishes or two extensive tasting menus, with most folks opting for one of the latter (if you're going to eat at Pinchiorri, you might as well go all out), the chef's tasting menu (€225, not including wine pairings) or the more-limited grand tasting menu (€190, not including wine). The chef's menu consists of eight courses. You might start with foie gras marinated in coffee and cooked in salt, or shrimp stuffed with pancetta and bay leaf. The appealing primi might include dishes such as *tortelli* stuffed with mashed potato and salt cod, or *pici* (thick homemade spaghetti) with sea urchin. The secondi are refreshingly rustic for such an haute kitchen, including chunks of suckling pig roasted on skewers and lamb loin stuffed with porcini mushrooms and *lardo di Colonnata*. Desserts are less regional and more avant-garde, such as a "peach soup" with almond gelato and tea gelatin. The à la carte menu offers langoustines in curry sauce, marinated asparagus, *spaghetti alla chitarra* (handmade squared-off spaghetti) with *bottarga* (dried mullet roe) and fresh tomatoes, and duck breast in spices, among other dishes.

Although the food is certainly over the top, it takes a backseat to the wine. Giorgio Pinchiorri's famed cellar is said to hold 180,000 bottles from Italy, France, and California—one of the finest collections in the world. Expert sommeliers, including Giorgio himself on occasion, will come to your table and suggest wines to accompany your meal. If you wish, they will suggest wines by the glass that can accompany each course.

Details like nineteenth-century antique furniture and huge bouquets of white lilies (the official flower of Florence) may even go unnoticed amid all the serious eating and drinking happening here. In the end, Pinchiorri's brand of gold-plated opulence is not to everyone's taste. But for those who are seeking excellent wines and imaginative Tuscan food in a setting of hushed elegance, look no further.

Teatro del Sale ✳

Via de' Macci 111r, 055/200-1492

Open daily; breakfast served 9 AM to 11 AM; lunch served 12:30 to 2:15; dinner served 7 PM to 8:45; music from 9:30 PM to 11 PM or so

€€

Map H4

Fabio Picchi of Cibreo and his partners have accomplished the truly admirable: they have created something original in tradition-bound Florence. With a mix of wicked humor, leftist politics, eclectic music, and Tuscan cooking par excellence, the Teatro del Sale is a special experience—a great evening of food and entertainment.

All diners arrive at the same time (7:30 PM) and are ushered into a huge warehouselike room that is somehow welcoming despite its size. You sit down at long tables with friends and strangers to eat incredibly good Tuscan cooking from a giant buffet. Grab your own plate to fill up on starters such as savory tarts and a variety of bean, grain, and vegetable salads, and bring back a selection for your friends (who'll surely repay the favor by making the next trip to the buffet once new dishes are brought out). The glass-walled kitchen lets you see everything that's coming out soon (huge pots of steamed mussels or clams, sausages, and other meats spinning on a rotisserie), and when a new dish is ready, the chef opens a little window and announces it to the diners at the top of his lungs. It's definitely more hectic than you might expect during a night out for dinner, but it's all part of the drama.

This is not the place to take a date, or to linger over every course. This is more like dinner theater, and the entertainment takes place both during and after dinner. When Picchi calls out dessert, in fact, you'd better hurry, because things run out. At the end of the meal, chairs are rearranged, tables are cleared (by the diners), and you're treated to a live musical performance. Some luminaries, such as Elvis Costello, have performed here, but more often the musical talent is local and can be classical, jazz, or cabaret, often of greatly varying quality. A schedule of the week's performers is usually posted on the front of the restaurant, though an explanation of what sort of show you'll see is not.

Teatro del Sale is based on the idea of a worker's union recreational club (*circolo*), and you have to "join" in order to eat here. The prices are not prohibitive, and you can join on the spot. A one-year membership is €10, but if you are just visiting you can also buy a cheaper (€5) nonresident membership, which is basically good for one use. Despite the membership charge, I consider the Teatro experience to be a bargain. Dinner is €25, including the excellent food, wine from the tap (not half bad), and the show. A light breakfast (€5) and lunch (€15) are also served, and you can linger a bit at both of them. This can be a pleasant, quiet place during the day to hang out, have a light snack, and browse the Italian and foreign newspapers and magazines that are set out for members.

Dining all'Aperto

When mid-July rolls around in Florence, it brings with it a hot sun and humidity that will curl your hair, make you wear unstylish shorts and sandals, and send you running for the nearest air-conditioned refuge. An even better solution is to eat your meals outside in a covered patio or piazza. Many local restaurants plunk a few chairs and tables on a busy street and call it a *terrazza*, but others are welcome retreats from the heat and traffic. Here are a few of the best places to eat outside in the center of town:

Osteria de' Benci, *page 44*

Borgo Antico, *page 115*

Quattro Leoni, *page 119*

Vecchia Bettola, *page 132*

Il Pizzaiuolo

Via dei Macci 113r, 055/241-171
Open Monday through Saturday 12:30 PM to 3 PM and 7:30 PM to midnight;
closed August
Map H4

This appealing pizzeria has a great location, right across the street from the Cibreo complex and the Sant'Ambrogio market. It has a nicer atmosphere than most pizzerias, looking more like an updated trattoria, with its weathered wooden chairs, marble-topped tables, and pretty green sign out front. The pizzas, cooked in a big wood-fired oven, have thick Naples-style crusts. However, the original Neapolitan *pizzaiolo* has moved to his own place, the Vico del Carmine (see page 133), so the pizza makers here now are actually Florentine. The basic Margherita is tasty, as is the *quattro formaggi* (four cheeses). Be sure to call for a reservation, as this is a popular spot.

Pizzeria Caffè Italiano

Via Isola delle Stinche 11r, 055/289-368
Open Tuesday through Sunday 7 PM to 1 AM
Map F5

The owners of Osteria del Caffè Italiano (see page 71) must have been homesick for a real Naples-style pizzeria, because they opened one right next to their reliable osteria. Savvy Florentines mainly use the bare-bones spot—basically just a huge wood-fired oven and about four wooden tables—for takeout, but you can also eat here. It's not a place to spend hours chatting with old friends, but it's ideal for a quick stop on the way to a movie, with a table pretty easy to snag before 8 PM. Like real Naples pizzerias, there are only three choices: Margherita, marinara (just tomato and oregano), and *napoletana* (with capers and anchovies), plus Coke and beer. The pizzas are thick, a little chewy, and authentic.

Lunching Like a Local

Many people in the United States, Britain, and many other fast-paced countries dislike their lunchtime options: an overpriced, overstuffed sandwich from the chain down the block; a greasy slice of pizza that you'll regret later; or a salad composed of ingredients that have been sitting out for hours. The other option is to sit down to a more substantial meal, although that can be heavy, pricey, and time-consuming. Wouldn't it be great if there were places where you could walk in and almost immediately be served a warm, delicious home-made meal that didn't cost much and didn't take up half your day?

Remarkably, there *are* places like that in Florence, and the locals wisely depend on them. They are not proper "restaurants" and don't provide fancy cooking—usually they put up a board listing three or four primi, perhaps two secondi, and some contorni—but they do deliver nourishing sustenance for great prices (usually around five euros per pasta) and eliminate any annoying formalities about eating

out. You have no obligation to order more courses than you want, and you generally order at the counter (sometimes the barman or cook will come around and ask). The pasta dishes are usually made up in huge pots, brought out, and served until they're gone. Nonetheless, the food is often excellent, and these places are filled with Italian businesspeople, students, construction workers, and everyone else who doesn't have a *mamma* nearby cooking lunch.

For the most part, these spots are casual bars or *pasticcerie* that have kitchens and serve only during the lunch rush, typically from 12:30 to 2 PM. They all have tables (inevitably filled), but the turnover is high, and with a short wait and bowl of pasta in hand, you'll be able to grab a seat fairly quickly. Most of these places are not in the Center and might not be necessary destinations for visitors on a short trip. But I'd be shirking my duties if I didn't tell you about them, because I and many other residents depend on them and never want them to disappear. Florence fortunately boasts a number of these lunchtime gems. Here are a few of the best:

Bar d'Azeglio
(Via della Mattonaia 55r, just east of Piazza d' Azeglio, 055/247-9263)
One of the most popular of them all—and rightfully so. Delicious pastas are served hot from large platters at the bar. Elbow your way up to the bar and be prepared to shout your order over the din.

Il Chicco di Caffè
(Via della Chiesa 16r, at Via delle Caldaie)
The owner's mother, Lola, is a terrific cook and has many admirers in the Santo Spirito area, me among them. She serves a short menu of pastas and secondi to order, which changes daily. This is a true neighborhood hangout, filled with local artisans and shopkeepers.

Bar Petrarca
(see page 143)
A great all-around bar and pastry shop at the Porta Romana with a popular and delicious lunch service in the back. The pastas are displayed in front and are usually a mix of hot and cold, with one rice or gnocchi dish, too.

Serafini
(Via Gioberti 168r, just east of Piazza Beccaria, 055/247-6214)
This friendly, bustling bar and pasticceria serves pastas and sandwiches at midday. Locals often finish off with a macedonia (fruit cup).

Enoteca Baldovino

Via San Giuseppe 18r, 055/234-7220
Open daily noon to 4 PM and 6 PM to midnight
Map G5

Across the street from the popular Trattoria Baldovino (page 70), this enoteca of the same name offers an abundance of wines by the glass and bottle, as well as some unusual light meals. Choose from a long list of *crostoni* (open-faced sandwiches) topped with every imaginable combination of cheese and vegetable, or a big salad with a wealth of ingredients. The menu also includes many different kinds of carpaccio, from meat to swordfish to vegetable, and a changing roster of daily pasta specials. The casual, subtly lit dining room plus bar up front has hardwood floors, and the walls, adorned with contemporary paintings by a local artist, are painted a pleasing ochre. This is a busy lunch spot, filled with international tourists weary after exploring the church of Santa Croce. Service can be slow when the place is at capacity.

Tavola Calda da Rocco

Inside Mercato Sant'Ambrogio
Open Monday through Saturday noon to 2 PM; closed part of August
Map H5

A *tavola calda* (literally "hot table") generally refers to an inexpensive place where the food is premade and kept hot, ready to serve. Florence doesn't have many *tavole calde*, which is just as well because they're usually not very exciting. The exceptional *tavola calda* in town is Da Rocco, a great stop for a cheap and unpretentious lunch inside the Sant'Ambrogio market. Possibly the best thing about Da Rocco is Rocco himself, a graying, slightly paunchy man with a great sense of humor who will tease you, flirt with you, and sometimes tell you what to eat. The food here is usually very good; I've eaten excellent *panzanella* and prosciutto with melon in the summer months, and in the winter I've hunkered down with Rocco's porcini risotto and stuffed eggplant. He is also famous for his lasagne and roast beef, which is served almost every day. *Panna cotta*, crème caramel, and other classic desserts are served, and prices are rock-bottom for Florence. In winter, wear a scarf because the market gets quite cold.

La Ghiotta

Via Pietrapiana 7r, 055/241-237
Open Tuesday to Sunday 11:30 AM to 3:00 PM and 6:30 PM to 10 PM; closed August
Map H4

Hungry Florentines head to this *rosticceria*, close to the Sant'Ambrogio market, for the savory roasted chicken and pork, steamed peas, sautéed spinach and other vegetables, and tempting thick-layered lasagne. It is unceasingly crowded here during prime lunch hours on weekdays. In the back are a few tables where you can sit and eat, or you can take out both hot and cold prepared foods.

COFFEE, CHOCOLATE, AND PASTRIES

Caffè Cibreo

Via del Verrocchio 5r, 055/234-5853
Open Tuesday through Saturday 8 AM to 1 AM; closed August, Christmas Day, and New Year's Day
Map H4

Part of the Cibreo food complex (see pages 72–73), this small café is decorated in the same dark woods and Parisian greens as the nearby restaurant and trattoria. Not many pastries are made here, but the ones that are made are good: usually just a brioche or two plus a special plum cake or unusual tart. This is always a fine stop for a cappuccino, and it's a way to capture a taste of Cibreo without the wait of the trattoria or the price of the restaurant. A light lunch is served in the daytime, and at night people sit at tiny round tables waiting to be seated in the other dining rooms, or sometimes eating meals from the restaurant kitchen here.

Words to Eat By

Babà = Small, leavened cake saturated in liquor and sometimes filled with cream

Bignè = Éclair

Biscotti(ni), cantucci(ni) = Hard Tuscan cookie, almost always made with almonds (the –ni suffix means they are extra-small)

Bombolone = Doughnut without the hole, often filled with custard

Brioche = Croissant

Budino = Dense pudding, often made with rice

Cenci = Fried dough covered with powdered sugar, served at Carnival time

Ciambella = Doughnut with the hole (or anything doughnut shaped)

Cornetto = Croissant (used less often in Florence than brioche)

Crema = Custard filling inside many pastries (cream in Italian is *panna*)

Frittelle = Sweet fritters

Gianduja = Mix of dark chocolate and hazelnut

Marmellata = Jam or jelly filling for many pastries

Mignon = Cream puff

Ricciarelli = Almond cookies from Siena

Schiacciata = Tuscan focaccia

Schiacciata alla fiorentina = Yellow cake flavored with orange peel, served at Carnival time

Torta della nonna = Custard tart topped with almonds or pine nuts (*tortina della nonna* is a smaller version that many Florentines take with their midmorning coffee; you'll sometimes see *tortina del nonno*, with chocolate, instead of vanilla, custard)

Patrizio Cosi ✳

Borgo Albizi 11r, 055/248-0367
Open Monday through Saturday 7 AM to 8 PM; closed August
Map G4

Cosi (pronounced "cozy") is the first word out of anyone's mouth when you mention pastries in Florence. As in, "Do you know what time the *bomboloni* come out of the oven at Cosi?" or, "Have you tried the chocolate brioche at Cosi?"

The place is instantly appealing, with a large glass case filled with delectable tarts, cookies, *babà al rhum*, and even a few savory snacks. I particularly love the tiny éclairs and tarts that are exactly the size of one bite. A refrigerated case near the entrance is filled with full-sized chocolate cakes, tremendous raspberry tarts, and *torte della nonna* that you can purchase to take home. At the marble-topped bar in back, crowds gather in the morning and afternoon to enjoy an excellent cappuccino or other coffee along with a pastry. Try the *cremino* (brioche filled with pastry cream) in the morning—it's the best in Florence. You'll also find a few tables and chairs where you can sit for a moment to recharge.

Staff at Patrizio Cosi.

Dolci & Dolcezze ✳

Piazza Beccaria 8r, 055/234-5458
Open Tuesday through Saturday 8:30 AM to 8 PM; Sunday 9 AM to 1 PM
and 4:30 PM to 7:30 PM
Map I5

Dolci & Dolcezze, with its lime green walls, marble counters, lace trim, and gilded moldings, looks like something out of a fairy tale. You could come just for a cup of Piansa coffee and a flaky, buttery croissant, but then you'd be missing out on a specialty that has made the shop a pilgrimage site for chocophiles—Giulio Corti's famous chocolate torte, either in party-sized rounds or little personal cakes dusted with cocoa powder. It's so rich that just a couple of bites will do, but you might as well eat the whole delicious thing. The little tarts filled with lemon curd or topped with raspberries or wild strawberries and powdered sugar are also excellent.

A few of the sublime cakes at Dolci & Dolcezze.

Gelateria Neri

Via dei Neri 20-22r, 055/210-034
Open daily noon to midnight
Map F6

Gelateria Neri has taken over where Vivoli, just around the corner, lets off: it's a little less touristy and a little less expensive than the older gelato grande dame. If you want to really indulge, try a cup or cone of the excellent coffee flavor, paired with chocolate or *nocciola* (hazelnut) and topped with a "correction" of whipped cream. The fruit flavors are equally appealing, especially in summer. The tiny shop is arranged so that you can lean against a kind of wall support but can't actually sit, which works out fine for the short time it takes to devour your gelato.

Veneta

Piazza Beccaria 7r, 055/234-3370
Open Wednesday through Monday 10 AM to midnight, 10 AM to 8 PM
in winter, 5 PM to midnight in August
Map I5

It's difficult to decide which flavors to choose at Veneta because everything looks good: try a delicious mix of *mirtillo* (blueberry) with a fantastically creamy *Buontalenti*. The *nocciola* (hazelnut) is superb, as is the chocolate, and they are great when paired. I also like the little treats for sale, including homemade ice-cream sandwiches and frosting-dipped cones. Special cakes to take away are lined up in the frozen case. Coffees are served from a small bar, but most people come here for the gelato.

Vestri

Borgo degli Albizi 11r, 055/234-0374
Open Monday through Saturday 10 AM to 7:30 PM; closed August
Map G4

Vestri is completely devoted to chocolate: chocolate candies, hot chocolate, and all kinds of creative variations on chocolate gelato—

chocolate-orange, chocolate-cinnamon, chocolate-mint, chocolate-*peperoncino* (hot pepper, a surprisingly good combination)—as well as pure, unadulterated chocolate. Vestri also sells its own beautifully packaged chocolates, which come filled with *gianduja*, walnut, coffee, puffed rice, and other flavors.

Vivoli

Via Isola delle Stinche 7r, 055/292-334
Open Tuesday through Saturday 7:30 AM to midnight, Sunday 9:30 AM to
  12 PM; closed for two weeks in August
Map F5

For a long time, this gelateria near Santa Croce has been considered the best gelato place in Florence. The gelato is indeed excellent, but customers should note that Vivoli's portions are a bit smaller and its prices a bit higher than at many other places. One reason to come here is for the terrific *riso* (rice) flavor; another is for the array of fresh fruit gelati—always a mix of mundane and unusual, like melon, kiwifruit, and blood orange—all vibrantly colored, pure, and delicious.

The fruit flavors at Vivoli.

Mercato Sant'Ambrogio ✳
Via dei Macci, Piazza Lorenzo Ghiberti
Open Monday through Saturday 7:30 AM to 1:30 PM
Map H5

Because it is smaller than the Central Market, Sant'Ambrogio feels a little less hectic and overwhelming. And although still within the old medieval circuit of walls, this neighborhood is a little farther from the Center, so it has a more local, less touristy feel.

Outside, on the Via dei Macci side (the front, if you're coming from the Center), you'll find a colorful quilt of seasonal fruits and vegetables. The farmers out to sell what they picked that morning—often only two or three things, like leeks and chicory—cluster on the far right end. Inside is a smorgasbord of cheeses, meats, dried beans, rice, and an excellent fishmonger. A daily flea market, held on either side of the building, is a good place to pick up cheap socks and towels, as well as flowers and plants.

Just inside the door on the Via dei Macci side, you'll see the excellent meats of **Macelleria Luca Menoni**; and on the north end of the hall, a stand called **Il Forteto** sells superb goat cheese (caprino), Gorgonzola, and a Parmesan-like aged cheese called gran sardo. Fish merchant **Fabio Gallerini**, located toward the northwest edge of the hall (these places aren't signed, so just look for the display of fresh fish), sells shellfish and a changing array of fillets and whole fish, such as cod (*merluzzo*), sea bass (*spigola* or *branzino*), and sole (*sogliola*). His selection is appealing, though not as abundant as what you find at the Central Market.

Mesticheria Mazzanti

Borgo La Croce 101r, 055/248-0663

Open Monday through Saturday 8 AM to 1 PM and 3:30 PM to 7:30 PM;
closed August

Map H4

Mesticheria Mazzanti is a busy, all-purpose hardware and home store. It offers a big selection of inexpensive kitchen goods, such as glasses, mugs, silverware, cheap pots, and wooden implements of all kinds—all of them useful for setting up a temporary kitchen. It's often crowded, so take a ticket and wait to be helped. You can enter the store either on Borgo La Croce or from Piazza Ghiberti (where the Sant'Ambrogio market is).

McRae Books
Via dei Neri 32r, 055/238-2456
Open daily 9 AM to 9:30 PM
Map F6

A married couple, one Florentine, one New Zealander, started a small English-language publishing company in Florence called McRae Books before they opened this clean, well-lighted bookstore of the same name. They stock an impressive collection of cookbooks, including by such authors as Carol Field and Michelle Sciccolone, in addition to their own titles, mainly by local authors.

5

SAN LORENZO, SAN MARCO, AND SANTA MARIA NOVELLA

In Florence, neighborhoods are usually named for the local parish church. The exterior of the church of San Lorenzo is rough and unfinished, but the interior is an iconic Renaissance masterpiece designed by Brunelleschi. San Marco, a little to the north and east, boasts a monastery filled with unparalleled frescoes by Fra' Angelico. The church of Santa Maria Novella is one of the most beautiful landmarks in Florence: the façade was designed by Leon Battista Alberti, and the inside is graced with frescoes by Fillippino Lippi, Ghirlandaio, and others. Not bad for your local parish. Here, for the sake of simplicity, I have bundled these three distinct neighborhoods on the north side of the historic center into a single chapter.

San Lorenzo is home to the Mercato Centrale, Florence's culinary nerve center. And **San Marco** has a few treats of its own. Both neighborhoods bustle with students, Florentine and foreign, which explains why you'll find few fine restaurants but an abundance of inexpensive places for meals and snacks. The neighborhood of **Santa Maria Novella** has been dragged into the hurly-burly of modern times by the train station, built in the 1930s. The neighborhood is now home to a fair number of Florence's ethnic shops and restaurants, as well as plenty of classic trattorias.

San Lorenzo and San Marco

RESTAURANTS AND TRATTORIAS

Trattoria Mario ✳
Via Rosina 2r, 055/218-550
Open Monday through Saturday noon to 3:30 PM; closed most of August
€
Map E2

My first meal in Florence was at Mario, which gave me an unrealistically inflated view of all future eating in the city. Décor is somewhere between simple and nonexistent, service is straightforward, the menu includes the same items as most other trattorias in Florence, and only lunch is served. You sit elbow to elbow at tables with whomever you are told to, and you like it! Mario has been discovered and is now listed in most guidebooks, including the *Slow Food Osteria Guide* (in Italian) but is still extremely welcoming, with brothers Fabio and Romeo, sons of the original Mario, running the place with good humor. It is popular with foreigners and locals, including businesspeople and professors from the university, some of whom eat here every day.

For primi, both the soups—*ribollita, zuppa di farro, zuppa di fagioli*—and the pastas—*amatriciana* (pancetta, tomato, hot pepper), *tagliatelle al ragù*—are consistently incredible: hearty, savory, pure in flavor. Mario is also one of the best places to try a real *bistecca alla fiorentina*, though the other veal and beef dishes, such as a plain fillet of beef or juicy *vitello arrosto*, are perfectly cooked as well. The *patate fritte* are outstanding, as is the mixed salad: it is no more than a bowl of lettuce and tomato dressed with olive oil, a drop of vinegar, and salt, and yet somehow it always tastes especially good, due either to the freshness of the produce or some kind of Mario X factor. Friday is fish day, when practically every item on the menu has some kind of seafood: pastas, salads, secondi. Dessert is usually biscotti and *vin santo*, if you have room. The house wine is drinkable, but there is also a longer wine selection. I don't want to hype this place out of all proportion, but when people ask me to name my favorite restaurant in Florence, I think of Mario. Then I get hungry.

La Festa dell'Unità

Every August, the few Florentines who have not fled to the beach or the mountains head to the Fortezza da Basso, an enormous open-air stone pentagon that was once Florence's military stronghold, for the Festa dell'Unità. The annual carnival–food fair–dancing-and-music party has political roots: it was long sponsored by Italy's Communist party as a celebration of both different cultures and working people. The *festa* is now sponsored by L'Ulivo, a softer center-leftist group, and by the leftist newspaper *L' Unità*. The politics are still here, but this is also an easygoing free carnival where you can wander around on a warm summer night and check out Indian scarves, Communist literature, and all kinds of international cooking. Many Italian and non-Italian restaurants and bars set up booths, including the restaurant India of Fiesole, Cuban and Moroccan eateries, a smokin' Argentinian barbecue spot, and several gelaterias and beer gardens. Late at night, the place fills up with people who come to dance and hang out. Mainly, this is a great chance to sample some different foods, drink beer, and listen to bad live music—what more can you ask for on a hot summer night?

PIZZERIAS

EDI House
Piazza Savonarola 8r, 055/588-886
Open daily 7 PM to 1:30 AM; closed August
Map H1

Most pizzerias on the outskirts of town flaunt their divey, down-and-dirty atmosphere—part of the whole pizza-and-a-beer experience—or they look like a Neapolitan version of elegance circa 1965. But EDI House on Piazza Savonarola is a little more chic and modern. The menu includes a full lineup of primi and secondi in addition to the pizzas. The *penne alla crema di olive e rucola*, with a creamy, tomatoey sauce and raw arugula leaves spread on top, is terrific. The kitchen also prepares stock favorites like *spaghetti alla carbonara* and *alle vongole* (with clams). The secondi favor skewered meats. The thin-crust pizzas come with a wide choice of interesting toppings, among them one with *prosciutto cotto* (cooked ham) and porcini, and another with capers, *prosciutto crudo*, and mozzarella. I love arugula on pizza, and the Margherita with arugula and shaved grana tastes great washed down with a cold stein of Tuborg beer. The house wine is a surprisingly good *vino sfuso* (from a big vat instead of a bottle).

SANDWICHES, SNACKS, AND LIGHT MEALS

Nerbone ✳

Mercato Centrale, first floor, 055/219-949
Open Monday through Saturday 7 AM to 2 PM; closed part of August
Map E2

Nerbone is more than a sandwich vendor, it's a contact sport. Your first challenge is to make eye contact with the man behind the cash register. If you succeed, you will be allowed to hand over about €2.50 in exchange for a receipt and go on to obstacle number two, the sandwich mob. You make your way over to the bullying, hungry crowd as they watch the man behind the counter make his famous sandwiches. What you want is called a *bollito* (boiled beef), *bagnato* (dunked in the meaty juices), with *tutte le salse* (both the spicy red and refreshing green sauce). But first you have to shuffle, insinuate, muscle, and connive your way to the front of the line. Or you can come early, before the noon lunch crowd arrives.

Nerbone also serves good pastas, an admirable *ribollita*, fresh salads, and meats such as a side of roasted chicken, but the real reason to come is for the sandwich. They also serve sliced *lampredotto* (fourth stomach), but I usually stick with the *bollito*. At times it can be fatty, but it's always good and goes especially well with an ice-cold Coke.

Oliandolo

Via Ricasoli 38r, 055/211-296

Open Monday through Saturday 10:30 AM to 10 PM; closed most of August and Christmas Day

Map F3

A crush of people clamor for the few wooden tables in this unpretentious lunch spot right between the Duomo and the Accademia. The small menu usually features a changing selection of primi, such as *spaghetti all'amatriciana* or *farro* salad. You can also move straight to a light secondo, such as roast beef with mashed potatoes or *vitello tonnato* (thin-sliced veal with tuna sauce, a specialty of Emilia-Romagna). Or, you can opt for one of Oliandolo's *insalatone*, a "big salad" featuring a variety of ingredients, or even an interesting vegetarian main, like a frittata with spinach, mozzarella, and grana. There's a small selection of good wines by the glass, the ideal complement to a small lunch between sights.

Pugi

Piazza San Marco 10, 055/280-981

Open Monday through Saturday 8 AM to 8 PM (Saturday 8 AM to 2 PM in summer); closed part of August

Map F2

Any Florentine will tell you that Pugi makes the best *schiacciata* (see page 27) and *schiacciata* pizza in town, and in case you still had any doubt, check out the mad rush of people flanking this place from well before lunchtime until it closes. This clean, inviting bakery makes perfect *schiacciata* with oil and salt in a wood-fired oven. You can get it unadulterated or in pizza form, covered with various toppings: thin-sliced zucchini, tomato and basil, truffles. Some beautiful breads and a few fruit pastries and sweet rolls are also available, but the people practically breaking down the door come for the *schiacciata*. Pugi is on the city's main bus-transfer spot, as well as in the middle of different university faculties. The original location, on the outskirts of town (Viale de Amicis 49r, 055/669-666), east of the Center, is undoubtedly a calmer eating experience. A third outpost, on Via San Gallo, has also been added.

Bussotti

Via San Gallo 161r, 055/483-091
Open Monday through Saturday 8:30 AM to 1 PM and 4 PM to 7:30 PM; closed
most of August
Map F1

The Bussotti family has run this tidy, comfortable wine shop, located just north of the Center, since 1935. Most of the stock is high-end bottles from Tuscany and Piedmont, including a generous selection of Supertuscans and Brunellos. The wide choice of good Chiantis includes Querciabella, Brolio, Villa Vistarenni, and Castello di Ama. Among the bottles of Brunello, you'll find Col d'Orcia, Castelgiocondo, and some smaller producers. The front room holds a broad stock of grappa, *vin santo*, and even French Sauternes.

Casa del Vino

Via dell'Ariento 16r, 055/215-609
Open Monday through Friday 8:30 AM to 3 PM and 5 PM to 7:45 PM, Saturday
8:30 AM to 3 PM; closed most of August
Map E3

Like Zanobini around the corner (see opposite), here is a narrow, good old-fashioned place outside the Central Market where you can duck in, sample a glass of wine, munch on crostini or other snacks, and duck back out blinking into the sunshine, all without sitting down or spending more than about five euros. Different wines are featured on different days, but you can count on seeing respected labels from Tuscany, Piedmont, and Friuli. Among the reds you might find a Morellino di Scansano or an Umbrian Merlot, and the whites are equally well chosen.

Zanobini

Via Sant'Antonino 47r, 055/239-6850
Open Monday through Saturday 8:30 AM to 2 PM and 4 PM to 8 PM
Map E3

Florence was once home to many spots like this old-school wine bar run by brothers Simone and Mario Zanobini, but now such establishments are a dying breed, replaced by fancy sit-down affairs. Like the stand-up coffee bars, this is meant to be the kind of place where businesspeople can stop in between meetings, or on the way home for dinner, for a glass of Chianti or Nobile for under three euros—nothing fancy or time-consuming. Zanobini also sells its own label of inexpensive wine, plus it stocks several tall shelves with mostly Tuscan reds, so if you like what you're tasting, you can also buy a bottle.

COFFEE, CHOCOLATE, AND PASTRIES

Nannini

Via Borgo San Lorenzo 7r, 055/212-680
Open daily 7:30 AM to 8 PM
Map E3

From outside, Nannini looks just like any other crowded, touristy coffee bar, but on closer inspection you'll find it's the Florentine outpost for tasting the specialty cookies of Siena. Many of the excellent biscotti made at this longstanding bakery contain soft, sweet almond paste, including the sweetly named *ricciarelli* (curlicues) and the *brutti ma buoni* (ugly but good). They sell the cookies in prepacked boxes, which make for nice gifts.

Carabé

Via Ricasoli 60r, 055/289-476
Open daily 9 AM to 1 AM
Map F3

Carabé's Sicilian owners make excellent fruit and nut gelati. The almond, walnut, and pistachio flavors are all standouts, and the perfectly tart-sweet lemon is the most refreshing thing you can eat on a hot summer day. They also make a deliciously creamy and slightly tart yogurt gelato, as well as fig—with fruit straight from the Central Market—when in season. People will tell you to try the granitas here, either coffee, almond, or lemon, but I have found them a little disappointing.

MARKETS AND SHOPS

Mercato Centrale ✳

Piazza del Mercato Centrale
Open Monday through Saturday 8 AM to 2 PM
Map E2–3

This hulking nineteenth-century structure was built as Florence's central market, and it, along with Mercato Sant'Ambrogio (see page 89), continues to serve as one of the city's best and least expensive places to buy a wide variety of fresh meats, fish, cheeses, and produce. On the ground floor, you'll find the meat, poultry, fish, *salumi*, and cheese—it's almost too much to take in, and not for the squeamish, as you'll occasionally run into a bloody lamb carcass, and always plenty of tripe and other offal. The selection of cheeses from all over Italy can be dizzying. Downstairs is also home to the lunch and sandwich spot **Nerbone** (see page 96) and a couple of other outlets for coffee and sandwiches, though the market's sometimes damp and chilly interior isn't always the most appealing place to linger.

The excellent seafood stalls cluster to one side of the first floor, and together offer by far the best choice of fish and shellfish in the city. The

The Baroni gourmet cheese and salumi *stall at the Central Market.*

numerous fruit and vegetable vendors, which are concentrated upstairs, are also among the best places in the city to find specialty herbs like dill and cilantro, as well as dried fruits and nuts. The competition among stands selling essentially the same items keeps prices down: if one apple seller has priced his apples too high, his customers can just walk across the hall.

Among the meat sellers, **Macellerie Soderi, Ieri,** and **Del Soldato** all have first-rate reputations. **Baroni** (055/289-576), located to the left when you enter from Via dell'Ariento, has a beautiful selection of Italian and French cheeses, as well as a host of *salumi* and an array of appetizing jarred condiments. In the same area, you'll find **Pasta Fresca,** where huge sheets of fresh pasta are cut into the shape of your choice while you wait. Il **Forteto,** a cooperative that produces meat and cheese, sells a nice range of pecorino cheeses, honeys, and selected *salumi* from a stand on the Piazza Mercato end of the first floor. If you just follow all your senses, you're bound to do well here. Even if you aren't in the market for a veal shoulder or a wheel of pecorino, it's still worthwhile to come in and look around. You will gain both a good sense of local raw ingredients (as well as some imports) and inspiration for future cooking endeavors.

Season's Eatings

In Florence's markets and restaurants, eating seasonally isn't a trend, it's a fact of life. If you really try, you could probably track down strawberries shipped from South America in winter or fava beans in fall, but why would you want to when they look rather pitiful next to the abundant local seasonal fruits and vegetables? There are some exceptions to this rule: Italians love imported pineapples all year long, and there's nothing wrong with the occasional mango. In general, however, it's best to eat what's naturally plentiful at the time.

Spring

Spring is the time to make the most of fava beans, artichokes, and asparagus. Most good pastry shops boast their *schiacciata alla fiorentina* (a cake, not the focaccia-like bread) before and after Carnival time in February and March, and around Easter they'll have such special treats as *frittelle*, fritters with rice or custard inside.

Summer

With the hot weather comes the best fruits: cherries, grapes, watermelons, peaches, and berries. It's also the time for peppers, eggplants, zucchini flowers, and, of course, tomatoes—big, fleshy red ones to be sliced into salad or mashed to sauce, little *ciliegini*, or lumpy *fiorentini*. Toward midsummer you can sometimes find early figs and small tart plums.

Fall

Figs make a cameo appearance from early to mid-September, so stock up while continuing to enjoy good tomatoes, peppers, and other summer produce that lingers into the fall. In September, market vendors compete to sell their fresh porcini mushrooms, and later, in November, prized white truffles from Umbria will pop up on menus at some city restaurants. By early December, sharp new Tuscan olive oils start to appear on the shelves. You'll also start to see plenty of *cavolo nero* and local apples from nearby farms in late October.

Winter

The apples and pears of winter are decent enough, but each week I regularly go through several kilos of the seedless *clementini*, tangerines that ward off winter colds. Winter is the time for spinach, all types of onions and bitter greens, *cavolo nero*, and Savoy cabbage. It's also hunting season, so you will see more *cinghiale* (wild boar) and *lepre* (hare) on menus around town, along with lots of local chestnuts. Christmas brings the dense, nut-filled *panforte*, as well as *panettone*, the big, puffy top hat–shaped bread filled with raisins and candied fruits.

ViviMarket

Via del Giglio 20–22r, 055/294-911
Open Monday through Saturday 9 AM to 2 PM and 3 PM to 7:30 PM
Map D3

Vivi is a small international supermarket, and perhaps the best thing to happen to expats living in Florence since the introduction of Laundromats. Here you can buy the staples of several Asian cuisines, including basmati rice, garam masala, and spices such as cumin, cardamom, coriander, mustard seeds, and fenugreek for Indian food; rice paper, hoisin sauce, and many things I have never heard of for Chinese and Vietnamese cooking; and such hard-to-find fresh ingredients as galangal and lemongrass for Thai food. Homesick Americans can fill up their carts with Jif peanut butter and Duncan Hines cake mixes, and Brits abroad will take solace in Marmite and Colman's mustard. (To top it off, American candies such as Nerds and Gobstoppers are stocked next to the cash register.) ViviMarket also sells woks, fry-strainers, and a small selection of ceramic dishes.

Look but Don't Touch

As tempting as it is to squeeze the tomatoes, shake the melons, and inspect the winter greens, try to hold back, as you might get your hand slapped by an indignant Italian vendor. In fact, at some markets you'll see English signs that say Do Not Touch, to guard against clumsy handling of fragile produce. For better or worse, Italians don't get to pick out their fruit and vegetables, and they believe it is unhygienic to let just anyone lay hands on them. Of course, this also means that while choosing your apples or lettuce, the vendor gets the chance to unload some less-than-perfect merchandise. A word of advice: It is not considered rude, and is in fact almost expected, that you will watch carefully as your fruit and vegetables are picked out, and you are well within your rights to say "that one please" and "not that [brown, bruised] one, please." Florentine matrons demand the best produce, and so should you.

RESTAURANTS AND TRATTORIAS

Cento Poveri

Via Palazzuolo 31r, 055/218-846

Open daily 12:30 PM to 3 PM and 7:30 PM to 10:30 PM (closed lunch Monday and Tuesday); closed two weeks in August

€€€

Map C4

It seems ironic that although many Florentines recommend Cento Poveri as one of the city's best restaurants, it is often filled with foreigners. Nonetheless, the recommendations are apt. Cento Poveri serves excellent food in a warm and inviting atmosphere, with casual décor and knickknacks hanging from the ceiling.

Delicious, slightly unusual primi, like *tortellacci* (big pasta pockets) filled with potato puree in a mushroom and chickpea sauce and lobster pasta with tomato sauce, come in surprisingly large portions. The tender and flavorful *bistecca alla fiorentina* is excellent. The grilled duck breast with a sweet brown sauce is also good, though the slightly heavy sauce threatens to drown delicate arugula leaves on the plate. Service here is friendly and the wine list is priced to drink, with plenty of appealing Chianti and Montalcino and Montepulciano reds for sale.

Il Latini

Via dei Palchetti 6r, 055/210-916

Open Tuesday through Sunday 12:30 PM to 2:30 PM and 7:30 PM to 10:30 PM

€€

Map D4

Perhaps you can't be too rich or too thin, but you can be too famous. The line snaking out the door at all hours of the day and night lets you know that Il Latini's greatness has been hailed in every guidebook from Hong Kong to Helsinki. It's so popular because it is exactly what many people want when they come to Florence: a lively, casual joint with satisfying Tuscan food. The raucous atmosphere, complete with Chianti *fiasco* bottles and hanging ham hocks, jokey staff, and classic food keep them coming. You might want to try lunch instead of dinner, when you're less likely to need riot gear in order to get through the door and the waitstaff is less likely to sling food at you, whether you ordered it or not.

The especially good crostini taste like they were dipped in butter before being slathered with succulent chopped liver. Excellent roast beef and *bistecca alla fiorentina* are a better bet than the *arista* (roasted pork), which is also a thick portion, but too salty. High-quality *ribollita* and *pappa al pomodoro* are served, too. Finish your meal off right with *biscottini* and terrific *vin santo*, made from grapes from the proprietor's own vineyard.

Parione

Via del Parione 74–76r, 055/214-005
Open Wednesday through Monday 8 PM to 11 PM; closed part of August
€€€
Map D5

Entering Parione, you might think you've walked in the wrong door, as you nearly step on the chef's toes and need to stay clear of plates flying off the stainless-steel kitchen counters. It is definitely an unusual entrance for a high-end restaurant, but it does give you an early peek at what's happening in the kitchen—the bustle of activity, good-looking slabs of meat, and nicely presented plates are all on display.

Parione has two dining rooms, both tastefully outfitted with ochre walls, shelves lined with wine bottles, and crisp white table linens. As customers arrive, the place fills up with happy chatter (almost all in Italian) and clinking wineglasses, while candles cast a warm light over the whole scene. Antipasti range from the classic combination of crostini and thin-sliced *salumi* to a more complex *sformatino di verdure*, a tasty mound of chopped spinach and chard accompanied with frothy hollandaise. The choice of primi is likewise a mix of the usual and the chef's fantasia: you can have a classic *ribollita*, a beautiful plate of *taglierini* with artichokes and herbs, or a plate of *caramelle*, little candy-shaped stuffed pastas filled with spinach and ricotta and topped with a peppery pork *ragù*.

Parione is known for its fish, but the secondi offer a selection of meat dishes, too. The beef fillet en croute is an incredibly rich concoction of steak, chopped liver, and pastry crust. In contrast, the fillet of *spigola* (sea bass) is delicately sauced with a creamy shrimp broth. Desserts might include a ricotta soufflé or an extremely dense slice of flourless chocolate cake. Unlike the menu, the wine list is a bit disappointing, filled with expensive bottles (strange given how untouristy this place is) and very slim on offerings for under thirty euros.

Sostanza
Via del Porcellana 25r, 055/212-691
Open Monday through Saturday noon to 3 PM and 7:30 PM to 10:30 PM
€€
Map C4

Here is a classic no-nonsense Tuscan trattoria, complete with gregarious owners (it seems the whole family works here), utilitarian lighting, and butcher shop–style white tile walls. The kitchen is famous above all for its *bistecca*, a huge steak grilled to bloody perfection. Sostanza also offers a reliable *ribollita* in winter, though you could easily skip over most of the unspectacular primi here and move straight to the secondi, settling on either the already-lauded *bistecca* or a chicken breast simply sautéed in (lots of) butter and served while still sizzling in the pan. A plain salad of arugula or radicchio acts as a refreshing complement to all that meat.

Sostanza has gained a reputation among foodies, both locals and out-of-towners, and you'll find snapshots of luminaries posted on the walls. Unfortunately, this also explains the relatively high prices for the rather simple fare (and atmosphere) and ordinary house wine. But I still recommend Sostanza for an authentic and rustic meal, especially at lunchtime when the fluorescent lighting is less annoying.

Beyond Bistecca — International Food in Florence

No one comes to Florence to eat *kung pao* chicken or baklava, but for the beleaguered expat, the adventurous local, or even the homesick traveler, these forays into international cuisine can be welcome. Here are a few to try, for snacks and full meals:

Amon
(Via Palazzuolo 26–28r, 055/293-146)
If you don't mind eating on your feet, Amon is a terrific quick stop for lunch or a snack. Get in line and choose among kebab, falafel, or *shwarma*.

Dioniso
(Via San Gallo 16r, 055/217-882)
A lively, updated version of a Greek taverna in the student-filled area near the Central Market.

Eito
(Via dei Neri 72r, 055/210-940)
Florentine date spot offers expensive but very fresh sushi in a sleek atmosphere.

La Habitacion Liquida
(Borgo Ognissanti 87r, 055/280-922)
Brightly painted and high-spirited place to stop for a light Spanish lunch or *aperitivo*.

India
(Via Gramsci 43a, Fiesole, 055/599-900)
Decent northern Indian fare in a fun, colorful, and romantic atmosphere in Fiesole.

Momoyama
(Borgo San Frediano 10r, 055/291-840)
Good, expensive sushi in a superchic minimalist atmosphere. The many rooms include a back patio covered by big, white canvas umbrellas and lit by flickering votives.

Nin Hao

(Borgo Ognissanti 159r, 055/210-770)
The best of the Chinese restaurants in Florence. Try the steamed dumplings, *kung pao* chicken, or spicy shredded pork with mushrooms. Wash it all down with a cold Tsingtao.

Rose's

(Via del Parione 26r, 055/287-090)
This supertrendy bar and Florentine date outpost serves fine sushi at high prices.

COFFEE, CHOCOLATE, AND PASTRIES

Becagli

Borgo Ognissanti 92r, 055/215-065
Open Thursday through Tuesday 6:30 AM to 2 PM and 5 PM to 8 PM,
Wednesday 6:30 AM to 2 PM; closed most of August
Map C4

You know you're in the right place when you see the line of Florentines snaking out the door, patiently waiting to squeeze inside and buy bread and *schiacciata* fresh from the oven or the perfect *torta della nonna*. The cookies filled with chocolate and hazelnut and the little semolina tarts covered with ruby red strawberry sauce are tops here. This place is abundance itself, overflowing with cookies, fruit pies, and savory breads and *pizzette*—a rare equilibrium between *forno* and *pasticceria*. There's no bar, but an unconnected place next door serves coffee and cappuccino if you need a pick-me-up. If you're here on Monday, Tuesday, or Saturday between 9 AM and noon, go and see Domenico Ghirlandaio's *Last Supper* in the refectory next to the Church of Ognissanti, right down the street.

Veneziano
Via dei Fossi 53r, 055/287-925
Open Monday through Saturday 9 AM to 2 PM and 5 PM to 8 PM, Monday
through Friday in summer
Map C4

Although the front-window display now features more jewelry than kitchenware, inside, Veneziano specializes in the kind of chic, modern kitchenware for which Italy is known. The shop has a particularly well-chosen selection of designer Murano glass dishes and bowls, as well as cut-glass wine stems, and porcelain pieces from brands such as Yalos, Driade, and IVV. If you want to send something home, Veneziano uses an expensive shipping service, so you may be better off carrying your purchases with you or shipping it yourself. The staff are helpful and speak fluent English.

BOOKSTORES

B & M Bookshop
Borgo Ognissanti 4r, 055/294-575
Open Monday to Saturday 9:30 AM to 7:30 PM, Sundays in summer
Map C4

This small English-language bookshop is the oldest in Florence, dating back to before the Arno flood of 1966. Current owner Cosetta Boni is usually in the shop and is knowledgeable about the inventory. She is happy to help customers find a book on the shelves or she'll order what you need. The store stocks a well-chosen selection of cookbooks and guidebooks about Tuscany and Italy.

A waiter outside Casalinga.

6

OLTRARNO

Oltrarno means "*oltre l'Arno*," or "the other side of the Arno" from the center of town. I have always been partial to this less-trammeled bank, which includes important monuments of art and architecture and, of course, gastronomy. For simplicity, in this chapter I have grouped together four distinct neighborhoods, each with its own character.

The **Santo Spirito** neighborhood is anchored by the Pitti Palace and Piazza Santo Spirito. This long rectangular piazza is fronted on one side by Brunelleschi's butter-colored Renaissance church and on the other with a series of graceful sixteenth-century palazzi.

Food lovers also have reason to head here. A mostly young crowd gathers at **Cabiria** (Piazza Santo Spirito 4r, 055/215-732) for an *aperitivo* on the patio. A few doors down, the agile *bariste* at **Caffè Ricchi** (Piazza Santo Spirito 10r, 055/282-864) make some of the best cappuccinos in town. Farmers and retailers sell fresh produce most days of the week, and on one Sunday every month, the piazza hosts an organic market, with everything from organic apples and pecorino cheese to batik scarves.

The neighborhood of **San Frediano**, just west of Santo Spirito, was once famous for its working-class toughness. It still retains much of its old character, but San Frediano is now more famous for both its old-school and newly chic restaurants than for its crime rate. Piazza Tasso, one of its main squares, has been rehabilitated, and it now houses not one, not two, but three fine restaurants and a great gelateria.

San Niccolò is almost too small to be considered a neighborhood. It consists of a few little streets that sit close to the Arno at the foot of the Ponte alle Grazie and then climb up toward scenic Piazzale Michelangelo. But although its footprint is small, this attractive, untrammeled part of town has its nice share of great restaurants and bars, including a classic trattoria and one of the city's best combination wine bar and restaurants.

If you continue south from Santo Spirito, eventually the old city walls of Florence come to a sharp point at the imposing **Porta Romana** (Roman gate). Although a little out of the way, it is worth braving the traffic-clogged roundabout outside the *porta* to explore the fruits of this unpretentious neighborhood, which include two great *pasticcerie* and one of the best pizzeras in town.

SANTO SPIRITO

RESTAURANTS AND TRATTORIAS

Beccofino
Piazza Scarlatti 1, Lungarno Guicciardini, 055/290-076
Open Monday through Saturday 7:30 PM to 11:30 PM, Sunday 12:30 PM to 2:30 PM (in summer) and 7:30 PM to 11:30 PM
€€€
Map C5

When it opened in 2002, Beccofino, with its blond woods, bold geometric shapes, and flatteringly dim lighting, was the first restaurant in town with a sleek architectural interior. But the look is no longer novel, and founding chef Francesco Bernardelli has been stolen away by Alain Ducasse. The cooking now focuses more on Tuscan dishes with a little international flair, such as stuffed porcini to start, followed by pumpkin ravioli and roasted monkfish or a *bistecca* of real Chianina beef from Falorni butchers in Chianti. But the cost is high and the atmosphere a bit too un-Florentine to be compelling to visitors. Owner David Gardner is a smart restaurateur, and in my opinion he will have to make some innovations in the menu, the service, and perhaps even the atmosphere before Beccofino can regain its former popularity. On the plus side, the wine list, heavy on Tuscan favorites, is well chosen and very reasonable.

Borgo Antico

Piazza Santo Spirito 6r, 055/210-437
Open daily noon to 3 PM and 7 PM to 11 PM
€€
Map C6

If Borgo Antico were located anywhere else, I would probably not recommend it. But its outdoor patio right on Piazza Santo Spirito is so pleasant and fun for lunch and dinner that I am giving it a pass despite indifferent service, sloppy pastas, and ridiculous pricing for daily specials. At least the portions are generous: mounds of gnocchi with tomato sauce, acres of pizza, seafood coming out of your ears. The pizzas from the wood-fired oven, including a classic Margherita and choices like spicy sausage with eggplant, are good if not always memorable; the linguine with clams is respectable; and I've seen diners get ecstatic over the huge platter of risotto with stracchino cheese and zucchini flowers. If you are thinking of ordering a secondo, try the lamb chops with roasted potatoes.

Borgo San Jacopo

Borgo San Jacopo 62r, 055/281-661
Open Wednesday through Monday 7:30 PM to 10:30 PM
€€€€
Map D6

I usually shy away from fancy hotel restaurants, as they often have unoriginal menus (and high prices) geared toward tourists. Borgo San Jacopo, which opened a couple of years ago on the street of the same name, is an exception. It is filled with stylish Florentines out on dates, in addition to well-heeled foreigners. Attached to the luxurious Lungarno Hotel (both are owned by the Ferragamo family), Borgo San Jacopo stands up on its own, showing flair in atmosphere, food, and service.

The long and narrow dining room with high ceilings is done mostly in white—white linens, white wooden wainscoting—in a way that is elegant and contemporary but not trendy. There is a great view of the Arno from the huge window at the end of the room, and a tiny loftlike space with about four tables up a flight of stairs. Both the host and the waitstaff are refreshingly friendly and helpful.

Chef Beatrice Segoni brought her whole team with her when she began cooking here. One of her specialties is a fish stew *alla marchigiana*, which arrives brimming with huge pieces of fish and shellfish in a small amount of tomato-infused broth. The menu leans heavily toward fish. For an antipasto, you can start with something "continental," such as a nicely made tuna tartare, or something local, like the traditional combination of *baccalà* and chickpeas. Primi range between interesting fish-oriented pastas and soups and well-executed classics like *bucatini all'amatriciana*. As a secondo, you might try a golden fillet of turbot served with roasted potatoes, or a good old-fashioned *bistecca*, if you haven't yet had your fill of meat in Florence. The wine list is extensive, as you would expect from a serious restaurant, but there are plenty of reasonable bottles, including a memorable Tocai from Friuli that goes well with the fish dishes. If you are looking for a place to celebrate a special occasion, or just to enjoy an elegant meal in the center of town, you won't be disappointed.

Casalinga

Via dei Michelozzi 9r, 055/218-624
Open Monday through Saturday noon to 2:30 PM and 7 PM to 10 PM; closed August and Christmas week

€

Map C6

One definition of *casalinga* is "housewife," and since most of us will never have or be one, this casual neighborhood place is the next best thing. Much loved by both locals and visitors, this is the kind of restaurant where people come to chat, catch up on the gossip and soccer news, and eat extremely cheap and basic food. The large no-nonsense interior, with big communal tables and red-and-white-checkered tablecloths, is almost always full and bubbles with life at both lunch and dinner. The best primi include lasagne, *ribollita* served in a hot ceramic pot, and simple dishes of spaghetti with piquant pesto or *aglio e olio*. The secondi, especially the grilled and roasted meats, are usually better than the primi.

Slow Food in Florence

The Slow Food movement wasn't born in Florence, but the city has of the biggest and most active *convivia* (chapters) in Italy. Every month, the Florence chapter organizes a flurry of wine and food-related activities. Visitors who would like to attend an event should check the website, www.slowfoodfirenze.it. Unfortunately, the site is mostly in Italian at the moment, as are most of the activities. However, wine and food can act as a kind of universal language.

Every other year Slow Food Italy hosts the Salone del Gusto in Turin, a food and wine festival and conference extravaganza. Toscana Slow, a regional celebration of Tuscan food that takes place over about a week in several cities and towns, happens on the years when there is no *salone*. To find out more about these regional and national events, and Slow Food in general, visit the organization's main website, www.slowfood.com.

₁ wonderful grilled pork chop (*braciola di maiale*) arrives adorned only with a wedge of lemon. Salads are ridiculously simple: shredded arugula or radicchio in a metal bowl. Order the *bollito misto* only if you are prepared to see a big pink tongue (along with other boiled meats) on your plate, ready to be sliced and doused with tangy green sauce. The house wine is a decent Chianti Rufina, and almost as cheap as water.

La Mangiatoia
Piazza San Felice 8–10r (Via Romana), 055/224-060
Open Tuesday through Sunday noon to 3 PM and 7 PM to 10 PM
€
Map C7

This clean, modest *rosticceria*-restaurant serves tasty roasted chicken, flattened under a brick and charred over an open flame, and many prepared sides, like roasted potatoes, eggplant, peas, and spinach. It also offers a rich lasagne with a hint of cinnamon and a good homemade tiramisù. Hidden in back is a dining room for anyone who wants to sit and eat an inexpensive pizza, a dish of pasta, or a plate of one of the roasted meats. Overall, this is a convenient full-service eatery and take-away for folks who live in the area or are looking for a snack near the Palazzo Pitti or Boboli Gardens.

Olio & Convivium
Via Santo Spirito 4r, 055/265-8198
Open Monday through Saturday 11 AM to 7 PM
€€
Map C5

The front room offers gleaming displays of cheeses, *salumi*, and prepared foods that can be taken home (for a price). In the back, you'll find a tranquil series of rooms where you can enjoy a light lunch (in air-conditioned splendor in summer), made from some of the same stellar ingredients. Although the the ambience is a little staid and the prices high, Olio & Convivium feels like the tenets of the Slow Food movement—simplicity, high-quality ingredients—being brought to life. You can order from the changing daily menu or opt for the tasting menu. The latter includes platters of specialty *salumi* from Cinta Senese (see page 26) and fine cheeses paired with *mostarda*. But you'll also find such *primi* as spaghetti with *bottarga* (cured mullet roe), and such classic *secondi* as roast chicken or pork. For dessert, a *millefeuille* with whipped cream and peaches is hard to resist. (The original location of Convivium, which is takeout only, is in the Gavinana suburb, Viale Europa 4–6, 055/681-1757.)

Quattro Leoni

Piazza della Passera, Via Vellutini 1r, 055/218-562
Open daily noon to 2:30 PM and 7:30 PM to 11 PM
€€
Map D6

Quattro Leoni, with its comfortable atmosphere, good service, and appealing menu, is one of the most enjoyable all-around trattorias in Florence—the kind of place where I always feel confident taking visiting friends and family. Lately it has become more expensive and touristy, and the kitchen may take some shortcuts, but I still recommend it on the whole.

You can start with a plate of *carpaccio di bresaola*, bright red, paper-thin slices of cured beef topped with shaved Parmesan, arugula, and pine nuts. Also popular is soft-pink prosciutto next to a mound of bufala mozzarella. A favorite primo is the *fiocchetti*, little "purses" of pasta filled with an intriguing mix of pear, asparagus, and Taleggio cheese. The kitchen also serves an impressive plate of *maltagliati con fiori di zucca*, "badly cut" fresh pasta in green and white with zucchini flowers, and gnocchi topped with a colorful pesto of arugula with fresh tomato. The best secondi are the plainly grilled meats, such as *tagliata* (sliced steak), veal chop, or a half chicken, all served with lemon wedges. If you still have room, try the cheesecake or the *panna cotta*, a disk of sweet cream topped with wild berries. Quattro Leoni's interior is a sprawl of brick-walled rooms with soft lighting and substantial charm, but the best way to enjoy this place is in the warm-weather months when you can sit outside in the quiet, nearly traffic-free piazza.

Il Santo Bevitore

Via Santo Spirito 64–66r, 055/211-264

Open Monday through Saturday 12:30 to 2:30 PM and 7:30 PM to 11:30 PM
   (closed Saturday lunch)

€€

Map C5

Although it boasted plenty of quality restaurants, the Santo Spirito neighborhood was lacking a place where you could sit down for a glass of good wine and a light bite. Then along came Il Santo Bevitore, which skipped over the usual settling-in period, becoming immediately popular. The spacious vaulted room with red tile floors is tastefully decorated with white-washed walls, custom-built shelves for wine bottles, and a large wooden bar along one wall. The atmosphere is casual and collegial (though loud); locals gather and chat at the dark wooden tables at lunch, and at dinner the room is softened by candlelight.

On the limited lunch menu, you can choose from tasting plates like a trio of paper-thin slices of first-rate prosciutto, *finocchiona*, and pancetta; and an arrangement of mixed cheeses. The kitchen also makes salads, including spinach with pine nuts and pears and a *nizzarda* (Niçoise salad). At night, the more extensive dinner menu might feature four or five hot primi to choose from, as well as several unusual secondi. The primi might be a risotto with zucchini, *pappa al pomodoro*, or something equally straightforward. The secondi, on the other hand, are a big departure from your usual roasted and grilled meats. On a given night your choices might include some odd yet successful dishes such as a parfait of winter squash and celery with tomato jelly, or a plate of thin-sliced fried calamari. The wine list includes about ten interesting wines by the glass, while the elegant selection by the bottle focuses on Tuscany and Piedmont. With fair prices, good wines, and a rustic-chic atmosphere, Santo Bevitore is perfectly suited for a lighter meal—the kind of neighborhood place you can drop into day or night.

Happy Meals

In general, Florentine restaurateurs are welcoming to children, but some casual restaurants and pizzerias in particular are better than others. It helps if the place is already a little noisy and raucous, and if you can get dinner earlier. Most restaurants do not have highchairs, though some do. If you're planning a visit you might want to bring a portable one with you.

Here are a few places that are especially welcoming:

Casalinga, *page 116*

It's big, cheap, and casual, and the staff won't keep you waiting six years for *il conto*. Best of all, it has a baby seat that attaches to the table. Kids like the simple *spaghetti al pomodoro*, *al pesto*, and *alla bolognese*.

Il Latini, *page 105*

A big, lively place where nobody minds noise and a little running around. Delicious *ribollita* and *pappa al pomodoro* are treats for both parents and kids.

La Piazzetta, *page 152*

Eyeing the crowd at this popular pizzeria on the outskirts of town, you'd never know Italy has a declining birth rate. Highchairs are available.

Pitti Gola e Cantina
Piazza Pitti 16, 055/212-704
Open Tuesday through Sunday 9 AM to 9:30 PM; closed most of August
Map D6

Take a seat at the inviting marble-topped bar, or at one of the few tables scattered inside or—when it's warm—outside, from which you can look straight across at the Renaissance bulk of the Palazzo Pitti. The walls are covered with floor-to-ceiling shelves of bottles, beginning with high-end IGT wines on one end, progressing along to Brunello and Vino Nobile, rounding the corner to Chianti Classico, and finally reaching wines from other regions, whites, and dessert wines. A light plate of assorted Tuscan *salumi* and cheeses goes well with a glass of wine. Downstairs in a side hallway, Pitti Gola stocks a well-chosen selection of cookbooks in Italian, English, and German, including titles on wine and food published by *Gambero Rosso* and Slow Food.

Millesimi ✳
Borgo Tegolaio 33r, 055/265-4675
Open Monday through Friday 3 PM to 8 PM, Saturday 10 AM to 8 PM
Map C6

Housed in a sixteenth-century palazzo, Millesimi has the feel of a contemporary art gallery more than a wine shop. Come here when you're looking for a special bottle or want to try something interesting and new, not for a cheap everyday wine. The selections are divided into little islands of Supertuscans, Chianti Classicos, wines from Piedmont, and organic wines. The store's owner, Marie Parrocel Pirelli, is a transplanted Frenchwoman from Marseilles, so in addition to stocking most Italian regions, there are some French bottles. Best of all, the manager, Gianni (who speaks some English), is happy to spend the time to talk you through the various offerings; his suggestions are always spot-on, whatever your price range. The inventory is selective instead of exhaustive. I like to come here, chat with Gianni, and experiment, be it with a

Sangiovese-Merlot mix from an up-and-coming Tuscan producer or an earthy Primitivo from Puglia. The shop stocks reds and whites from Cusumano and Planeta in Sicily, and many excellent Reislings and Sauvignons from Trentino–Alto Adige.

Le Volpi e L'Uva ✳

Piazza dei Rossi 1r (off Via Giucciardini), 055/239-8132
Open Monday through Saturday 10:30 AM to 9 PM; closed most of August
Map D6

Although it's in prime tourist territory, just off the foot of the Ponte Vecchio, unassuming Le Volpi e L'Uva ("the foxes and the grapes," named after a fairy tale) has resisted the temptation to become fancy or fake. The tiny interior has only a dozen or so seats at the marble-topped bar and some room for standing, and in summer you can sit outside in the car-free piazza.

Giancarlo Cantini and his small crew of dedicated sommeliers and wine enthusiasts seek out only small, unknown producers from all over Italy in search of the holy grail of *un buon rapporto prezzo/qualità* (a just relationship between price and quality). They've done an exceptional job. Categorically ignoring overhyped big-name wines, they find new producers at various wine fairs, when traveling around for pleasure, or when friends or associates bring them wines to try. When a wine they serve becomes too famous and raises its price, they discontinue it, such is their dedication to bargain *bicchieri*.

The frequently changing chalkboard of wines by the glass lists about a dozen whites and reds, probably the most varied and interesting—not to mention well-priced—choice in the city. On a given evening, it might feature unusual wines from Alto Adige, including several reds from this area more associated with whites. Wine estate names don't appear on the chalkboard, but if you look behind you on the shelves, you can usually spot what you're drinking that night. While you drink, you can snack on little mixed plates of delectable *salumi* and cheeses that pair well with the wine.

Dolcissimo
Via Maggio 61r, 055/239-6268
Open Monday through Friday 9 AM to 1:30 PM and 4 PM to 7:30 PM, Saturday
    9 AM to 1:30 PM
Map C6

This little boutique of chocolates and other sweets is an impressive and relatively new addition to Via Maggio, a street known for its Renaissance palazzi and high-end antique shops. Stop here for a quick jam-filled cookie or a homemade chocolate. Or you can take home a mouthwatering chocolate cake or berry and cream tart. The shop belongs to the same people who own both Caffè Italiano (page 57) and Osteria del Caffè Italiano (page 71), and Alle Murate (page 43), and supplies some of the sweets for those restaurants, as well as a few others.

GELATO

La Carraia
Piazza Nizario Sauro 25r, 055/280-695
Open daily 10 AM to 11 PM; occasionally closed during winter months
Map C5

La Carraia has somehow escaped the notice of most Florentine food cognoscenti, but the gelato here is very satisfying. Fluffy, creamy, decadent, no-nonsense flavors like coffee, *nocciolosa* (combination of chocolate and hazelnut), and chocolate are all excellent. It even sells a delicious Nutella yogurt for those who aren't sure if they're on a diet or a binge, or ricotta and figs, for those who want to try more local flavors. You might go elsewhere, however, for your fruit flavors; here they are cream based and not as appealing as the water-based flavors at Grom (see page 62) or Carabé (see page 100).

Morganti

Piazza Santo Spirito 3r, 055/289-230

Open Monday through Saturday 8:30 AM to 1 PM and 4:30 PM to 8 PM in winter, daily 8:30 AM to 7:30 PM in summer; closed part of August

Map C6

This odd little store on Piazza Santo Spirito is worth knowing about for its dried grains, rices, and beans, which are sold in bulk from huge sacks. Some of the items are traditional, like *toscanelli* (white beans), *farro*, and Arborio rice, and some more difficult to find in Florence, such as black beans and wild and basmati rice. It also carries an eclectic assortment of organic goods for people and pets, a variety of straw mats, and baskets of all sizes.

Useful items on sale at Morganti.

RESTAURANTS AND TRATTORIAS

All' Antico Ristoro di Cambi
Via Sant'Onofrio 1r, 055/217-134
Open Monday through Saturday noon to 2:30 PM and 7:30 PM to 10:30 PM;
   closed August 15

€

Map B5

Cambi has all the ingredients necessary for success: a crowded clutch of bare-topped wooden tables and stools, a vaulted brick ceiling, the right noise level for eating and chatting with friends, warm lighting, and a drop-dead amazing *bistecca alla fiorentina*. The fact that *every single person* seems to be eating the *bistecca* rather than one of the other attractive secondi is the tip-off that this is no ordinary steak. The primi here are fine—a very Tuscan bean-laden *farro* soup, or the more unusual *pennette* with fresh ricotta and arugula—but basically serve as time-killers leading up to the main event. The enormous T-bone steaks are perfectly cooked (rare but not raw) and served no-nonsense on wooden platters. A side of roasted potatoes and a mixed salad go well with the beef. Other salads here are good but can be a little too do-it-yourself for my taste: one time I ordered fava beans with pecorino, only to be served a basket of unshelled beans and a hunk of cheese. (I later learned this was a special dish for May Day.) The only negative here is the house wine, which is poor. My best advice is to order a real bottle of red from the bar, even though you might be the only customer in the place doing so.

Le Barrique

Via del Leone 40r, 055/224-192
Open Tuesday through Sunday 8 PM to midnight
€€
Map B5

The owners here have put together a small but interesting menu and have created an inviting, intimate atmosphere. The tiny kitchen turns out mostly traditional Tuscan dishes, with some innovation thrown into the mix. Primi might include summery dishes like fresh tagliatelle with zucchini flowers and cherry tomatoes, while the secondi menu features both roasted meats, such as the classic *arista* (pork loin with herbs) and fillet of beef, and a good-looking eggplant Parmesan. The restaurant also has a pretty vine-covered garden in back, a tempting option for the summer months.

I' Brindellone

Piazza Piattellina 10–11r, 055/217-879
Open Thursday through Tuesday noon to 3 PM and 7 PM to 11 PM
€
Map B5

If you like what Florence offers in pastas and soups but can usually pass when it comes time for the secondi, you'll appreciate I'Brindellone. Here the owners have taken the basic concept of a no-frills trattoria but have dispensed with the obligatory stuff-yourself-until-you-drop three or more courses, focusing instead on what is often the best part anyway: a creative and extended list of tempting primi. The choices include a delicious spaghetti with *pomodorini*, sliced garlic, shredded basil, and shards of aged ricotta, and a bowl of *zuppa livornese*, mussels cooked in an aromatic mix of tomatoes, hot pepper, and garlic, with a sauce-soaked slice of bread at the bottom. The menu also features Parmesan and balsamic vinegar *gnocchetti* in a crispy cheese basket, and intriguing nettle-filled ravioli topped with basil. This is one of the best places in town for a carnivorous friend to take a vegetarian friend (or vice versa), without having to worry about being trapped by a menu full of tofu and bean sprouts or *bistecca* and brains, respectively.

Cavolo Nero

Via dell'Ardiglione 22r, 055/294-744
Open Monday through Sunday 8 PM to 11 PM; closed August
€€€
Map C6

This midsized restaurant, hidden in one of the more picturesque lanes between the Santo Spirito and San Frediano neighborhoods, offers a subdued and appealing interior in winter and a shady garden in summer. Tables are covered with crisp white linens, and even the chairs have been canvassed in white. The kitchen is clearly trying to create some unusual dishes, and for the most part succeeding. It's nice to see a menu that offers antipasti other than the usual prosciutto and crostini, such as scallops with quail eggs and bacon and roasted salt cod with herbs. The primi are more standard, like spaghetti with clams and *farro* soup garnished with a leek cake. Secondi diverge from the usual Tuscan chops and meats, offering a selection that includes fish (turbot and sea bass) and fowl (pigeon stuffed with foie gras). The wine list is excellent and features all price ranges.

Il Guscio

Via dell'Orto 49, 055/224-421
Open Tuesday through Sunday 8 PM to 11 PM; closed August
€€
Map A5

Il Guscio holds a position of high esteem among Florentines, a good reason to track down this San Frediano haunt. The interior is unassuming, with yellow walls, red tile floor, and no windows. But the locals don't love this place for its atmosphere. Instead, it's because they know they can sit down to true Tuscan flavors without breaking the bank.

Start with an *antipasto toscano*, a mix of crostini and *affettati* (sliced cured meats). The excellent primi include a fresh pappardelle with an

Where the Florentines Are

Sometimes Florence can feel like the fifty-first state of the Union, with more English than Italian spoken on the streets. Once in a while it's nice to go where the Florentines regularly eat. What they look for in a restaurant is *tipicità*, traditional Tuscan recipes cooked the way they should be. They like their roasted meats salty and their wine economical. Here are ten places where you can mix with the locals:

Il Guscio, *opposite*

Firenze Nova, *page 152*

Trattoria Mario, *page 94*

Fuori Porta, *page 138*

Sabatino, *page 131*

Santa Lucia, *page 153*

Targa, *page 149*

Il Tranvai, *page 132*

Tre Soldi, *page 150*

Vico del Carmine, *page 133*

incredibly rich and flavorful *ragù* of duck and white wine. As a secondo, many diners opt for the *bistecca* or *tagliata*, both done in the classic style. Solid, satisfying desserts include a disk of vanilla ice cream in a bowl of hot chocolate—a different take on the *affogato*—and a *crostatina di crema*, a delicious tartlet filled with fluffy pastry cream and topped with fresh fruit. The wine list includes substantial choices from Piedmont and Tuscany, as well as a couple of labels from Puglia and Sicily, all at fair prices. Friendly and helpful servers are yet another plus.

NapoLeone

Piazza del Carmine 24, 055/281-015
Open daily 7:30 PM to midnight
€€
Map B5

San Frediano is already a gold mine of well-liked restaurants, and yet there always seems to be room for one more. The owners of NapoLeone, a sprawling, stylish place popular with young Florentines, put quite a bit of thought—and money—into the décor of their combination trattoria and pizzeria. The many dining rooms feature vaulted ceilings, flagstone floors, and nicely outfitted tables with big, clubby chairs. In summer, a large outdoor seating area is set up on the piazza. There is even a private room decked out like a hunting lodge, with wood paneling, a fireplace, and stuffed animal heads on the walls. I've never seen anything quite like it in Florence.

Although the food won't bowl you over, this is a fun place to dine, especially with a group of friends. The menu includes a list of pizzas and a surprisingly generous selection of primi and secondi. Despite the nod to Naples in the restaurant name, the pizza is not quite Naples style, and is actually disappointing. You are better off sticking to the primi and secondi, such as a satisfying taster plate of Florence's favorite soups (*pasta e fagioli*, *ribollita*, and *pappa al pomodoro*) or a simple pasta dish, followed by fillet of beef, grilled rare, or one of the fish dishes. You can get inexpensive wines by the glass, such as a Morellino di Scansano from Moris Farms, or you can choose a bottle from the mostly Tuscan wine list, which includes everything from a lowly house red all the way up to Opus One, with plenty of reasonable choices in between.

Pandemonio

Via del Leone 50r, 055/224-002

Open Monday through Saturday 12:30 PM to 2:30 PM and 7:30 PM to 10:30 PM; closed August, Christmas Day, and New Year's Day

€€€

Map B6

Pandemonio skirts the line between classic trattoria and elegant restaurant. The menu is hearty Tuscan cooking, with some standard primi, such as *ribollita* and *pappa al pomodoro*, alongside more inventive offerings, including fresh *pasta al ragù*, spaghetti with *bottarga* (dried mullet roe), and house-made *tortellacci* (large pasta pockets) with a Gorgonzola and radicchio sauce. Secondi tend to be on the heavy side, with the classic Florentine steak served either whole, for two people, or in slices (*tagliata*) with either arugula and balsamic vinegar or artichokes and Parmesan cheese. One of the best reasons to come here: the chocolate and cheese cakes are considered some of the best in the city.

While the menu is basic and unassuming, the atmosphere and prices aspire to greater things. Hushed conversation (largely in foreign languages) fills the dining room, soothingly done in yellow linens and candlelight. The wine list offers a respectable choice of *spumanti*, Champagne, and local vintages. You won't go wrong with one of the Chianti Classicos, such as Badia a Coltibuono, or a similarly priced bottle of Morellino di Scansano.

Sabatino

Via Pisana 2r, 055/225-955

Open Monday through Friday noon to 2:30 PM and 7:30 PM to 10:30 PM; closed August, Christmas Day, and New Year's Day

€

Map A5

The initial impression of Sabatino as a bare-bones spot, with its industrial-strength fluorescent lighting and long plastic-covered tables, is confirmed by its being one of the cheapest places to eat in town, with primi hovering at about four euros and secondi at just a couple euros more. In itself this wouldn't be a recommendation, but the food is quite good. The menu is utterly basic: spaghetti with tomato sauce, spaghetti with meat sauce, tagliatelle with tomato . . . you get the idea. I've enjoyed several meals here of *farro* soup, roast beef with potatoes or *pancetta di vitello*, and house wine. The owners are friendly, and it's not hard to get a table at the last minute, even with a large group. The location, too, is fairly convenient, just outside the Porta San Frediano in the Oltrarno.

Il Tranvai

Piazza Torquato Tasso 14r, 055/225-197

Open Monday through Friday noon to 2:30 PM and 7:15 PM to 10:45 PM; closed August, Christmas Day, and New Year's Day

€

Map B6

Il Tranvai is beloved by locals, and the atmosphere is fun and low-key, though the food can be hit-and-miss. Like other no-frills Florentine joints, this one is noisy and tightly packed at mealtimes. The popular mixed crostini plate—a cute little wooden tray of toasts topped with artichoke, tomato, and chicken liver—is usually very satisfying. Among the primi, I've enjoyed the pasta with tomato and spicy sausage but was disappointed in a walnut gnocchi and a vegetable soup. The secondi are traditional: tripe, chicken, pork, and beef, with the pork meatballs in tomato sauce especially tasty. One atypical aspect of Il Tranvai is its excellent selection of house-made desserts. Wine here is extremely reasonable, and the atmosphere is convivial and truly *fiorentino*.

Vecchia Bettola ✳

Via Ariosto 34r (Piazza Tasso), 055/224-158

Open Tuesday through Saturday noon to 2:30 PM and 7:30 PM to 10:30 PM; closed August and Christmas week

€€

Map A6

Vecchia Bettola, owned by the same family that presides over Nerbone (page 96), home of the legendary *bollito* sandwich in the Central Market, is one of the best old-school trattorias in the city. Here, you sit on wooden stools and benches, drink wine out of a giant straw-wrapped *fiasco*, and wolf down *ribollita* and *bistecca* with gusto. The special pasta of the house, *penne alla Bettola*, is made with a tomato and vodka sauce that is wonderfully sweet and delicious. Other outstanding primi are the rigatoni with olive and roast-tomato sauce, and creamy risotto dishes.

The secondi, contorni, and salads are usually admirable as well, with plenty of unadorned grilled steaks and chops of pork, beef, and veal. The kitchen serves a celebrated *bistecca alla fiorentina* and a decadent osso buco (wintry but served year-round). Even the simple *insalata mista* outshines similar dishes around the city. The outside seating is terrific in summer, when the bustling interior can be too hot. One caveat: save your coffee stop for after dinner; there's no espresso machine here, so all you can get is Nescafé in little tin cups.

PIZZERIAS

Vico del Carmine ✳

Via Pisana 40–42r, 055/233-6862
Open Tuesday through Saturday noon to 2:30 PM and 7:30 PM to 10:30 PM
Map A4

You don't see too many decorated "theme" restaurants in Florence, perhaps because the whole city is a kind of medieval-Renaissance theme park. But Naples is foreign enough from the bourgeois calm of Florence to merit its own theme, and an enterprising and food-loving family from Campania has created this little reproduction of a Naples *vicolo* (alleyway), complete with fake hanging laundry and business signs. Luckily, what they have also reproduced is top-quality Naples-style pizza and friendly and knowledgeable service. Owner Carmine is the former *pizzaiolo* at the restaurant Il Pizzaiuolo (see page 79) next to Mercato Sant'Ambrogio. Here, he makes his wonderful pizzas in a huge, igloolike wood-burning oven, the likes of which you rarely see outside Naples. The rest of his immediate and extended family are either busy in the kitchen or manning the tables and phone.

The restaurant has a complete osteria menu with an equally authentic focus on fish. You could start with a big bowl of steamed mussels, or a more local plate of delicious thin-sliced *salumi*. If you are not having a pizza, try the pasta with clams or scampi, or fresh fish for a secondo. But the main reason to come here is for the pizzas, with their thick, puffy crust and low middle. Try the classic Margherita, or for a true taste of Naples, the *friarielli e salsicce* (bitter—seriously bitter—greens with sausage). All of the pizzas look, smell, and taste great, and they are all large and filling. If you have room for dessert, order the *panna cotta* with caramel sauce, or a shot of real *limoncello*. Vico del Carmine is popular with Florentines, who know a good pizza when they taste one, so make sure to reserve ahead.

COFFEE, CHOCOLATE, AND PASTRIES

Hemingway
Piazza Piattellina 9r, 055/284-781
Open Tuesday through Saturday 4:30 PM to 1 AM, Sunday 11 AM to 8 PM
   (brunch 11:30 AM to 2:30 PM); closed August
Map B5

Hemingway is primarily a nighttime destination, with hot drinks, from various hot chocolates to coffee drinks to a long list of teas, the focus. You'll find cocktails, too, and a nice selection of locally made chocolate candies. The menu offers a choice of puddings and cakes and a platter of assorted candies from Slitti, a top chocolatier in Monsummano Terme (see page 61), and from Paul De Bondt of Pisa, another leader in the field. Even a regular coffee comes with a little spoon made of fine chocolate and cocoa. Stop in for a late-afternoon coffee or hot chocolate after you visit the Brancacci Chapel in the church of Santa Maria del Carmine, just down the block. On Sunday, doors open early for a big brunch.

Sunday Brunch

Sunday brunch has become popular in Florence, even if the concept has changed in translation. Forget about blintzes and an omelette with bacon. Instead, several places now offer big buffet-style lunches around noon on Sundays. Some serve Anglo-American breakfast fare such as cereal, toast, yogurt, and even eggs, but most serve some combination of Italian primi and international foods, with the focus on the prix-fixe buffet rather than traditional brunch cuisine. Most of the brunch places are also popular aperitivo bars.

Here are some of my favorites:

Fusion Bar, Gallery Hotel
(Vicolo dell' Oro 5, 055/272-669-87)
Brunch buffet featuring sushi, other items, and dessert served from noon to 3 PM on Saturday and Sunday; €25.

Noir (formerly Capocaccia)
(page 141)
Sunday brunch buffet from noon to 3 PM with breakfast foods and Italian primi and secondi; €20.

Il Rifrullo
(page 141)
Very popular brunch spot, where you can eat either inside or on the patio. Italian and international food served buffet-style at 12:30 PM on Sunday; €20.

Beconcini

Viale Pratolini (Piazza Tasso), 055/223-604
Open Monday 6:30 AM to 1:30 PM, Tuesday through Friday 6:30 AM to 8 PM,
Saturday and Sunday 6:30 AM to 2 PM and 4 PM to 8 PM
Map A6

I stumbled on Beconcini and was impressed with both the pride the staff takes in its product and the product itself. The family has been making pastries and gelato for over forty years and they know their craft. The *semifreddi* (half-frozen mousse made with cream instead of milk) are especially good here, as are the *gianduja* (chocolate with hazelnut) and *stracciatella* (chocolate chip) gelati. Beconcini closes early in the evening, so you see many Florentines here in the late afternoon buying big containers of gelato to take home, put in the freezer, and serve after dinner.

SAN NICCOLÒ

RESTAURANTS AND TRATTORIAS

Osteria Antica Mescita di San Niccolò

Via San Niccolò 60r, 055/234-2836
Open Monday through Saturday noon to 2:30 PM and 7:30 PM to midnight
€
Map G7

The Antica Mescita, in the heart of the San Niccolò neighborhood, is a fine neighborhood trattoria (even if it calls itself by every name except that one). The place is warm and friendly, with the usual beaten-up wooden tables, benches, and stools, and old photos and wine bottles lining the walls. The menu has not only all the staple comfort items but also a few more challenging dishes. The kitchen loves *lardo*—on crostini, as carpaccio—and tripe, and they always offer some surprising dishes like carpaccio of smoked goose breast. But you can also enjoy a great *ribollita* or a stunning rosemary-spiked *farro* and chickpea soup. I like almost everything served here, though in general I recommend the soups over the pastas. Secondi don't take a backseat either: I often get the thin-sliced *arista* with apple-prune compote, though I'm usually tempted by the various stews, too, such as wild boar with spices or beef with porcini. The menu changes at least slightly every day, including featured wines and cheeses. The house wine is a highly drinkable Chianti, but bottles are priced so reasonably that it's a good chance to try something else. And if you order a bottle, you get the thrill of watching the waiter use a "cherry picker" to pull it off the shelf above your head. For dessert, you can choose from among *affogato* (gelato doused with an espresso), assorted cheeses with honey, and other traditional sweets.

When you reserve, make sure you ask to be seated in the charming ground-floor room, to avoid the dark basement space, which is a bit dungeonlike. In summer, there's a pleasant little outdoor space with three or four tables, protected by bushes from scant passing traffic.

Filipepe
Via San Niccolò 37-39r, 055/200-1397
Open daily 7:30 PM to 1 AM; closed two weeks in August
€€€
Map G7

You now see a lot of young Florentines with a "Hey, let's give it a go" attitude toward opening a restaurant, and some have launched funky, bold eateries that draw large crowds of locals and tourists. Filipepe is among the best of this group, because the food and ambience add up to something more than a hip date destination (though it is certainly that). The front of the restaurant is decorated in an ersatz bordello style, with long, dramatic drapes and an eclectic mix of tables and chairs, though the professional service and pinpoint lighting keep it from looking like a tent at Burning Man. The back room and the patio boast a chic, more minimalist style and moody lighting, making both spots the best places to hang out, dine, be seen, and—if you are young and Italian—smooch, of course.

The food is a mix of local specialties with some experimentation and seafood. Your best bet for success is to choose from among the tried-and-true pasta and fish dishes, although even the failures (tuna tartare, for one) are not too bad. In general, antipasti are where chefs feel the most free to editorialize. At Filipepe, you should navigate these choices carefully, or else skip them altogether and head directly to the more straightforward primi and secondi. Large ravioli filled with white fish and topped with a mix of butter and *bottarga* (dried mullet roe) shavings are a hit. You also can't go wrong with something like *pici* (thick, long pasta) with *ragù* of lamb and artichoke. For your secondo, skip the tuna steak and focus on the fresh fish of the day.

Like some of the dishes themselves (anchovy flan with fava bean mousse, red pepper, and wild fennel, for example), the presentation is a little over the top, including plates the size of flying saucers, but I find the exuberance admirable. Save room for the desserts, especially the *mocha semifreddo* or lemon tart.

Fuori Porta
Via Monte alle Croci 10r, 055/234-2483
Open Monday through Saturday 12:30 PM to 3 PM and 7 PM to 12:30 AM; closed two weeks in August
€€
Map G7

This charming, casual wine bar and restaurant, popular at both lunch and dinner, is efficiently run by three partners. The menu is essentially ten pages of *crostoni*—open-faced sandwiches of melted cheese and other good things on toasted Tuscan bread—though it also has a short rotating list of good pastas dressed with seasonal sauces, such as zucchini flowers and *stracchino,* or *pici* (thick, long pasta) with mixed seafood. The secondi are mostly cold dishes, like carpaccio of beef or swordfish with arugula and a squeeze of lemon.

Call ahead and reserve at night; in summer, the best seats are on the patio, which looks down onto one of the medieval gates of the city (hence the name, which means "outside the gate"). The list of wines by the glass changes every two weeks or so and usually is a pleasing mix, with choices from Piedmont and other regions, as well as Chianti, Nobile, and IGT labels from closer to home.

I Tarocchi

Via de' Renai 12–14, 055/234-3912
Open Tuesday through Sunday 12:30 PM to 2:30 PM and 7 PM to 1 AM
Map F7

I Tarocchi has been around for ages, initiating American students abroad and others to the ways of good thin-crust pizza year after year. The quality of the pizzas may have gone down a bit lately, but I still think of this as a reliable place for a casual dinner. Some very good pastas, such as linguine with clams, are served in addition to pizza, and you can often get a table at the spur of the moment, which is a bonus. The main dining room has a laid-back feel, with long, wooden benches and posters of tarot cards (hence, the name). I usually order a pizza topped with Gorgonzola or a Margherita with arugula, along with a good lager from the tap and a nice big mixed salad of lettuce, tomato, and carrot. I Tarocchi is a ten-minute walk from Piazza Santa Croce, across the Ponte alle Grazie. If you still have energy after dinner, try one of the many bars in the neighborhood.

Aperitivo alla Fiorentina

The *aperitivo* hour—or hours, usually roughly from 7 to 9 PM—is a particularly Florentine pastime. It's a little like the American happy hour, except somehow more chic and fabulous. It's a chance for locals and in-the-know visitors to get dressed up before dinner (which happens late here), sit outside if it's warm, enjoy the sunset and the beautiful city, and socialize in style while sipping brightly colored concoctions.

The classic *aperitivi* are the Negroni (gin, Campari, sweet vermouth) and the Americano (red vermouth, Campari, and soda water), or a Prosecco or other *spumante* (sparkling wine). But most bars now also serve imports like margaritas, daiquiris, martinis, and caipirinhas, which, though departures from tradition, are great on a hot summer night.

The most popular *aperitivo* haunts put out impressive displays of food to go along with the alcohol. Many stick to crostini but others go further, with pasta salads, polenta, paella, even sushi. Some people have been known to cobble together a full meal from the offerings, which goes a long way toward justifying the bank-breaking price tag on most Florentine cocktails.

Here are some of the best places to enjoy an *apertivo*:

Dolce Vita
Piazza del Carmine, 055/284-595; open daily 11 AM to 2 AM
Located right next to the Chiesa del Carmine and the Brancacci Chapel, Dolce Vita was the in place in the early 1990s, went through a slight slump, and then relaunched with new owners and a design makeover about five years ago. It has been hugely popular ever since. The crowd here is stylish, mainly thirtysomething Florentines who come to chat, have an *aperitivo*, and check out what one another is wearing.

Gilli

Piazza della Repubblica 36–39r, 055/213-896; open Wednesday through Monday 7:30 AM to 10 PM; closed one week in August
If you want to sidle up to an art-nouveau bar serviced by a liveried *barista* and have your *aperitivo* in old-world style, here's the place. The drinking starts early—you'll sometimes see older Florentines sipping bright red Campari and soda before lunch rather than dinner—and the buffet spread is always impressive, brimming with a colorful assortment of olives, cheeses, and little sandwiches.

Noir (formerly Capocaccia)

Lungarno Corsini 12–14r, 055/210-751; open Tuesday through Sunday noon to 2 AM, closed part of August
Noir is a bar of superlatives: most fashionable clientele, best buffet of free food, and (unfortunately) worst attitude, both the staff and the Florentines who frequent the place. If you come early, you'll avoid some of the crowd and are more likely to get a table, or at least be able to elbow your way to the bar.

Caffè La Torre

Lungarno Cellini 65r, 055/680-643; open daily 10:30 AM to 3 AM
This is a trendy locale for young Florentines and expats to gather, both inside and on the shaded front patio. Drinks are expensive, but the customers don't seem to mind as they flirt and fill up their plates with the good free food at one of the most abundant *aperitivo* buffets in town.

Il Rifrullo

Via San Niccolò 55r, 055/234-2621; open daily 8 AM to 1 AM; closed two weeks in August.
I liked the old, preremodeled interior better, but the upstairs patio at sunset is one of the most suggestive and tranquil spots in Florence. Snacks are so-so, but the bar scene is fun. There is also a full restaurant menu.

PORTA ROMANA

PIZZERIAS

Antica Porta ✳
Via Senese 23r, 055/220-527
Open Tuesday through Sunday 7:30 PM to 1 AM

I lived up the hill from this pizzeria for three or four months before I noticed the crowd always waiting outside and then finally ate here. When I think back on the pizzas I could have consumed during those ignorant months, I quiver with regret. I no longer live in the neighborhood, just outside the Porta Romana on the southern tip of town, but Antica Porta is still my favorite pizzeria. Gravelly voiced owner Nello answers the phone and acts as host and cashier. He comes from Salerno, which explains the obsession with burrata (a soft cheese that combines mozzarella and caciocavallo) and bufala mozzarella.

The front room—its window always steamed up in winter—has just a couple of tables; but beyond you'll follow a skinny hallway to the back where the place opens up into a busy, boisterous dining room painted a pleasant ochre. You can't help but notice the roaring wood-fired oven up front where they make pizzas with the thinnest Roman-style crust in town: delicate, crunchy, crackerlike. The pizza menu is daunting, but try not to be overwhelmed by the choices—they are all good. Some of the best on the list are the Margherita with grana and basil; the pizza with bresaola and arugula; the specials with fresh tomatoes and bufala mozzarella; and the *fiori di zucca* with mixed cheeses. In summer, there is a delicious and exquisitely presented *prosciutto e melone* appetizer, or a plate of local prosciutto with burrata and a tomato relish.

Although this place is known primarily for its pizzas, the pastas are amazingly just as good. Try the *gran scoglio*, linguine tossed with mussels and clams cooked with garlic, parsley, and olive oil. If you see *gnudi* (little dumplings of spinach and ricotta) with a rich veal sauce on the specials board, order them. They come beautifully plated—a match for any three-star restaurant. *Tiramisù al caffè*, with amaretti instead of ladyfingers, is astonishingly good. If you have room, try one of the dessert "pizzas," pizza dough filled with Nutella and topped with gelato and chocolate sauce. Need I say more? Last, the service is friendly and helpful. The same hardworking staff people are here time after time, always attentive, happy to see me, and ready to translate a menu item or recommend a favorite dish.

COFFEE, CHOCOLATE, AND PASTRIES

Gualtieri
Via Senese 18r, 055/221-771
Open Tuesday through Sunday 7 AM to 1:15 PM and 4 PM to 8 PM;
closed August

Small, bustling Gualtieri is the place to come for a warm-from-the-oven flaky pastry filled with ricotta, a sweet rice fritter (*frittella*, an Easter specialty), or just a very good cappuccino and brioche. The specialty of the house is a *torta tirolese*, a semolina tart made with fresh pears, but everything is high quality here. The shop makes its own chocolate candies, and even sells chocolate bars with the house label. The place can be a little crowded, and the service is cordial, if not overly warm.

Bar Petrarca ✳
Piazzale di Porta Romana 6r, 055/221-092
Open Sunday through Friday 6 AM to 8:30 PM; closed August and
Christmas Day

This multifaceted bar fills several important functions: you can get an excellent cappuccino and pastry, a quick lunch of either pasta or one of the prepared foods in the glass case, or an afternoon éclair, or you can pick up an entire cheesecake, apple tart, or *torta della nonna* for a party, all made in-house and all terrific. (For the record, cheesecake in Italy means something slightly different than in America: it's more like a sweet quiche.) Best of all, Petrarca is open all day on Sunday (though closed on Saturday). The friendly *bariste* manage to prepare ten cappuccinos a minute during the morning rush with flair.

Tuscan cooking legend Benedetta Vitali.

7

OUTSIDE THE CITY WALLS

The medieval walls of Florence are mostly just a memory, with only the imposing *porte* (gates) demarcating the old routes in and out of the city. But their outline still forms both a theoretical and real frontier between the center and the periphery. The city center is filled with Rensaissance *palazzi*, museums, churches, hotels, money-changing shops, Internet points, restaurants, and tourists. It's old, it's romantic, and it's impossible to park or drive, which is why more and more Florentine families head out to the "suburbs," or even the still-urban but more modern areas outside the walls. Here, you'll find some of the most unspoiled, inexpensive, and authentic restaurants and trattorias. And most of the best gelato and pizza is served outside the city walls. Make the effort to visit a few of these places, and you will be well rewarded. Plus, the journey can be half the fun.

RESTAURANTS AND TRATTORIAS

Bibe ✳

Via delle Bagnese 1r (south of town, toward Scadicci), 055/204-9085
Open Thursday through Tuesday 7:30 PM to 10:30 PM, Saturday and Sunday
for lunch 12:30 PM to 2:30 PM

€€

When the birds are singing, the sun is shining, and the stone streets of Florence feel narrow and stifling, I can think of nothing better than lunch at Bibe, a short ride from town. Make sure to ask for a table in the leafy, tree-shaded garden if it's sunny. (In winter, you'll sit inside the charming farmhouse.)

Like most of the restaurants around Florence, Bibe is a family-run operation that hasn't changed much over the years, nor does it need to. The menu consists mainly of Tuscan standards but also includes a few unusual and expertly done specials and uncommon seasonal dishes. The old-school waiter might assume you want the house red, but take the time to look over the wine list, which offers a number of excellent whites and reds at prices barely higher than retail. On a summer day, you might start with a chilled Chardonnay from Alto Adige and then move on to a local red, such as a superb Chianti Classico from Fontodi.

Meals start off soundly, especially if you order the fried zucchini flowers—in season in spring and summer—stuffed with mozzarella cheese and fried in a light, luscious batter. Another antipasto features a fava bean salad with creamy goat cheese. For a primo, you might try the *papardelle al ragù di lepre*, fresh pasta with a savory wild hare *ragù*. Secondi include a range of roasted and grilled meats. The lamb roasted with potatoes comes as a petite but succulent portion wrapped in aluminum foil. Although the food is excellent here, the true beauty of this place is the magic atmosphere outdoors, where the sun glitters off pink tablecloths and sparkling wine goblets.

Omero ✳

Via Pian dei Giullari 11r (Arcetri), 055/220-053
Open Tuesday through Sunday noon to 2:30 PM and 7:30 PM to 10:30 PM
€€

Galileo's house arrest doesn't seem so cruel when you approach the gilded hilltop area where he was confined, in the village of Arcetri, just southwest of the city walls. It's about a ten-minute cab ride or forty-five-minute walk uphill from the Ponte Vecchio to Omero, and well worth the trip.

If it were down in the Center, Omero would still be an elegant restaurant serving classic Tuscan fare of high quality, but the reason to make the trip here is for the combination of great food, the blockbuster view, and calm country atmosphere. I recommend coming at lunchtime to experience the full spectacle. Omero's upstairs and downstairs dining rooms have tall windows on three sides overlooking a picture-perfect valley and old stone farmhouse across the way. In winter, double panes let in the light without the cold, and in summer, this place really shines, with a large outdoor seating area and gentle breezes blowing through. Ask to sit upstairs when you reserve; the view and light are a little better.

Start with an outstanding mixed antipasto plate, which includes some of the best crostini and *salumi* I've tasted, the latter sliced paper-thin and arranged in the little "shop" in the front entryway. The primi are ridiculously simple: choose a pasta (ravioli with spinach and ricotta, penne, or strand pasta), and then pick the sauce to go with it (excellent *ragù*, fresh tomato sauce, or a changing special). As a secondi you might opt for the *bistecca alla fiorentina*, sliced beef (*tagliata*) with arugula, or a grilled veal chop. The kitchen likes to fry, and specialties of the house include fried chicken and fried rabbit. The cooks never veer from Tuscan favorites, but since they do them so well, this isn't a problem. The accompanying wine list includes plenty of extraordinary, expensive reds, along with many reasonably priced choices (Chianti Classico, Carmignano, and other local wines). The trained sommelier will be happy to recommend a bottle.

Osvaldo
Via Gabriele D'Annunzio 51r (on the way to Settignano), 055/602-168
Open Thursday through Monday noon to 2 PM and 8 PM to 10 PM; closed
Wednesday dinner; closed August
€

We should all be so lucky to have a place like Osvaldo as our neighborhood restaurant. Run by the Righi family since 1978, Osvaldo is an old-school Florentine trattoria in the best sense: casual, welcoming, inexpensive, and full of regulars. The interior looks like a sprawling country house, and many of the rooms are decorated with portraits, bric-a-brac, and yes, even red-and-white-checkered tablecloths. In summer, diners can eat on a big covered patio. You're likely to see mostly Florentines here, plus some scholars from Harvard's Villa I Tatti, which is right up the road.

Osvaldo sticks to the standards, and with great success. The *tagliatelle al ragù, tagliatelle con porcini freschi*, and homemade *pici alla carrettiera* (tomato sauce with pepper flakes) are all terrific, though the best primo here is the *gnocchi della casa*: potato gnocchi in a tangy mushroom-tomato cream sauce. Secondi are equally satisfying: the *bistecca* is superb, served beautifully rare, as it should be. The fried rabbit, which can be extremely dry and disappointing at other places, is also a standout, dipped in a thick, savory batter and fried golden brown—crunchy outside with tender and juicy white meat inside. The wine list is almost non-existent—just a scant page of Chianti and Morellino di Scansano—and most diners opt for a liter of the house red, a respectable Chianti.

Da Ruggiero
Via Senese 89r, 055/220-542
Open Thursday through Monday 7:30 PM to 10:30 PM; closed August
€

This rock-solid trattoria serves authentic Florentine cooking at a reasonable price. The wood-paneled walls are decorated with a clutter of old prints and photos, and even a stuffed deer's head. There's nothing fancy or experimental here, just simple, classic dishes such as an excellent *ribollita* and *pappa*, memorable chopped liver crostini, and secondi that often include a fish or two. This is a good place to try a *pinzimonio*—a plate of raw vegetables that you cut up yourself and dip into extra virgin olive oil. The spicy *spaghetti alla carretiera* is cooked perfectly al dente and tossed with an *abbondanza* of fresh tomatoes, garlic, and *peperoncino*. Definitely call in advance to reserve, as the small place is often booked.

Targa
Lungarno Cristoforo Colombo 7 (Piazza Alberti), 055/677-377
Open Monday through Saturday 12:30 PM to 2:30 PM and 8 PM to 10:45 PM
€€€

Targa, formerly called Caffè Concerto, overlooks the Arno just east of town. Despite an incongruous entryway that looks like a disco, the restaurant is extremely inviting and romantic. (Due to its out-of-center location, it's said to be a popular spot with Florentines for their assignations.) Picture windows overlook the river, and there are plants everywhere.

The menu has a welcome focus on seafood. The antipasti are generally complex creations, such as a crepe of smoked salmon and salmon egg with a side of *finocchio* salad, or *culatello* (a prized form of prosciutto) served with braised marinated scallions. Your best bets among the primi are the various pastas with shellfish, such as an incredibly delicate and flavorful linguine sauced with shrimp, scallops, and parsley, or a *pasta alla chitarra* (thick, square-cut homemade spaghetti) with a spicy calamari sauce. Fish also dominate the secondi, including a dish of red mullet fillets served on a bed of Tuscan white beans. The beef cheeks braised in a sauce of Armagnac and basil, an upscale bourguignon cooked until the beef melts in your mouth, is immensely satisfying. The wine offerings are truly encyclopedic, with many whites from all over Italy that work well with the kitchen's seafood, as well as reds and some special dessert wines.

Tre Soldi
Via Gabriele D'Annunzio 4r (Campo di Marte), 055/679-366
Open Sunday through Thursday noon to 2:30 PM and 8 PM to 10:30 PM,
   Friday noon to 2:30 PM
€€

Tre Soldi is popular with locals, who come here for both the Tuscan classics and to try something a little different. It's in a nondescript part of town past the stadium, on the road toward Settignano, reachable by bus or by a long, but not picturesque walk from the Center. In winter, diners eat in the pleasant indoor rooms. When summer arrives, the action moves outside to the spacious covered patio, where dive-bombing mosquitoes can sometimes get in the way of full enjoyment of what otherwise feels almost like an elegant picnic.

For an antipasto, you can choose delicious crostini with liver or be a bit more daring: the *mocetta d'agnello*—cured slices of lean meat from the tail of a lamb paired with a fetalike cheese—is an unusual treat that I have seen only here. Try the *tortellini al ragù* or one of the other classic primi. The specialty of the house among secondi is the *tagliata*, and the sliced Chianina beef, perfectly cooked (rare) and served either with arugula or *lardo* and herbs, is indeed delicious. On the other hand, I find the thin-sliced *arista alla porchetta* soaks up too much oil for my taste. The dessert list is more extensive than at most trattorias, with a choice of unusual sorbets (lemon and sage, green apple and Calvados, melon and hot pepper) and equally odd gelati (pistachio with gin and pepper, cinnamon with balsamic vinegar).

Zibibbo *

Via di Terzollina 3r (Careggi), 055/433-383
Open Monday through Saturday 12:30 PM to 3:30 PM and 7:30 PM to midnight;
closed August

€€€

Zibibbo only seems to get better with time. Benedetta Vitali, an energetic Florentine who has dedicated her life to Tuscan cooking, helped create Cibreo (see page 72), perhaps the best-known restaurant in Florence, before opening Zibibbo in 1999, in the leafy suburb of Careggi. The short drive from the Center does not deter her admirers: the modern dining room, outfitted with skylights and contemporary Tuscan landscapes, is bustling with locals and foreigners at both lunch and dinner.

The menu is classic Tuscan with southern Italian and Mediterranean leanings. Start with outstanding fried zucchini flowers (in summer), or the kitchen's creative take on *crostini al fegato*, here a plate of briochelike bread served with two luscious fingers of fine liver paté and an orange zest confit. On a given day, primi might include *spaghetti alle sarde*, which marries sardines, raisins, and pine nuts, or a more Tuscan tagliatelle with duck sauce. The secondi always feature a choice of fish dishes and several interesting meat offerings, such as roasted pork with a purée of apples, and duck with a grape sauce. Definitely save room for dessert, as they are Vitali's claim to fame. The all-Italian wine list includes Tuscan leaders like Felsina and Castello di Ama, as well as up-and-coming makers from the south, all with reasonable markups.

Firenze Nova ✳

Via Benedetto Dei 122 (Firenze Nuova), 055/411-937
Open Monday through Saturday 7:30 PM to 11 PM; closed August

I entered Firenze Nova the first time as a jaded pizza connoisseur, unsure of what new twist this place could possibly show me. I had already tasted Florence's wood-fired offerings, from cracker-thin crusts that wobbled under the weight of cheese and sauce to thick Neapolitan-style pies with a lake of bufala mozzarella. I found the clean, modern interior (at the base of a Soviet-style apartment block) too brightly lit, but the Florentine couples and families that filled the place didn't seem to mind. That's probably because Nova is definitely one of Florence's best—if not its best—pizzerias. Naples-style crusts are just the right thickness and not too heavy (easily digestible, as Italians would put it). The best pies here are the *melanzane a sorpresa*, which comes with mounds of fresh ricotta, smoked mozzarella, thin-sliced sausage, and bits of roasted eggplant on top, and the Margherita DOC, with more smoked mozzarella. Pizzas are the main event, but the restaurant also offers a full menu of primi and secondi. A big plate of mussels, cooked in white wine and pepper flakes, makes an excellent antipasto or secondo.

La Piazzetta

Piazza del Bandino 43r, corner of Viale Europa (Gavinana), 055/680-0253
Open Wednesday through Monday noon to 3 PM and 7 PM to 1 AM

The one problem with most pizzerias in Florence is that a hot oven in a small, enclosed space can interfere with enjoyable dining, especially in summer. La Piazzetta, which lies east of the city center in the residential neighborhood of Gavinana, has solved that problem. The pride of La Piazzetta is a big outdoor patio with a retractable ceiling and surrounding shrubbery. This is also a family place in every sense of the word: family run, friendly vibe, kids running amok while gobbling down pizza and calzone.

La Piazzetta is also a full-fledged restaurant, offering classic antipasti like liver-topped crostini and prosciutto with melon. But most people come here for the pizzas, which are in the Naples style, with a hefty, crunchy crust. You'll find all the standards (Margherita, marinara, *funghi*) alongside some unusual picks, plus a wide choice of calzone, focaccias, and *covaccini* (pizza dough with oil, garlic, and choice of topping such as *lardo* or prosciutto—essentially a pizza without the sauce and cheese). The Napoli DOC is a good choice, with melt-in-your-mouth anchovies and capers, and the Gorgonzola pizza is pleasantly piquant. If you have room when you're done here, stop in at Il Sorriso gelateria (page 160) around the corner.

Santa Lucia
Via Ponte alle Mosse 102r (Porta al Prato), 055/353-255
Open Thursday through Tuesday 7:30 PM to 1 AM; closed August

Santa Lucia is about three or four blocks outside the Porta al Prato, on the west side of town. You can get here by bus or taxi, or you can walk, though the busy route is not particularly attractive. The pizzeria's big, noisy interior has been redone and is no longer *squallida* (bleak), as even its admirers used to describe it. The menu, perhaps also as a nod to all things *napoletana*, is heavy on seafood, and an appetizer of mussels in butter and garlic is outstanding. Many patrons order the good-looking primi, like spaghetti with clams and *rigatoni alla puttanesca* (spicy tomato sauce), and the meat and fish secondi.

The pizzas come either in thin Roman style (*basso*) or thicker Neapolitan style (*alto*), so diners have a choice. The eponymous Santa Lucia pizza is especially good, topped with *prosciutto cotto*, ricotta, and mozzarella. I also like the pizza topped with tomato, cheese, onion, and spicy sausage, and I like the *marinara*. Both the *alto* and *basso* pizzas are tasty—good crust, quality toppings—and best of all, this place is truly cheap, as pizza and a beer should be. Santa Lucia is one of the most popular pizzerias among locals, which means you should definitely reserve.

Pizzeria Spera

Via della Cernaia 9r (Fortezza da Basso), 055/495-286

Open Tuesday through Friday noon to 2:30 PM and 7 PM to 11 PM, Saturday and Sunday 7 PM to 11 PM; closed August

Salvatore Spera, the ex-boxer who runs this place, missed his calling as a heavy on *The Sopranos*, but you can still watch him, resplendent in white baseball cap and tanktop, muscles covered with tattoos, as he arranges pizzas for the oven behind a sliding glass window. Spera is originally from Naples, and he and daughter Elena serve *napoletana*-style pizza to the madding crowds.

You can call in advance to put your name down, but the staff doesn't seem to get the reservation concept, so the system is essentially first come, first served. The place draws lots of locals, mainly young Florentines whom you'll see spilling out of the tiny take-out section. Downstairs is calmer, with two rooms of wooden tables and benches and 1950s movie posters adorning the walls. Unlike most Florentine pizzerias, Spera only serves pizza—no salads, no pastas, just pizza. The offerings are a mix of tomato and *bianca* (white). I have found the tomato-based pies, such as a nice Margherita or a pizza with tomato and spicy sausage, are the best. Such no-tomato versions as potato and mozzarella, coupled with a Neapolitan crust's traditional thickness, can be too heavy.

Spera has achieved cult status, but the pizza is worthy of hoopla: you can taste the quality of the ingredients in the crust, the tomato sauce, and the fresh mozzarella. But what really makes the pizza here special is the crust, which is a hefty inch and a half thick around the outside. If you manage to finish your plate here, I'll be impressed. The pizzas are also incredibly cheap; you can easily get out of here for less than ten euros. On the way out, have a look at the photo of Spera in boxing mode and at his old gloves hanging from the ceiling.

I' Gottino

Via Gioberti 174r (Piazza Beccaria), 055/244-797
Open Monday through Friday 9 AM to 10:30 PM, Saturday 9 AM to 2 PM
Map J5

This bright, small sandwich shop near Piazza Beccaria attracts young professionals who live and work in the area. The choice of sandwiches, which come on *ciabatta* and *schiacciata*, includes salami and pecorino, tomato and mozzarella, or a custom combination. Well-chosen wines by the glass are an added bonus, as is the outdoor patio along Via Gioberti in the warm-weather months.

WINE SHOPS

Bonatti ✳

Via Gioberti 66–68r (Piazza Beccaria), 055/660-050
Open Monday through Saturday 9 AM to 1 PM and 4 PM to 8 PM; closed Monday mornings in winter; closed Saturday afternoon in summer
Map J5

Bonatti's two large rooms are full of shelves that are well organized and easy to browse. In addition to the superb array of Italian wines, you'll find a decent selection of wines from Chile, Australia, South Africa, and France, as well as crystal wineglasses, high-tech bottle openers, and other accoutrements. The focus, however, is always on the wine itself: everything from Supertuscans to grappas from Tuscany and the Veneto.

Buscioni

Via Centostelle 1r, (Campo di Marte), 055/602-765
Open Tuesday through Sunday 7:30 AM to 2 PM and 3 PM to 8 PM

Occasionally you'll see handwritten signs on the windows of *pasticcerie* that say *Bomboloni Caldi, 16:30* (hot doughnuts at 4:30 PM). Compared to wild boar salami or sandwiches with truffle oil, hot filled doughnuts are not an exotic novelty to the average traveler, but Tuscans really take to them (they even opt for hot doughnuts as a beach snack instead of something cold like a Popsicle), and Florentines will all tell you that Buscioni makes the best *bomboloni caldi* in town. I don't recommend a special trip to this out-of-the-way spot just for the doughnuts, but if you happen to find yourself near the Campo di Marte stadium around 4:30 PM, it's a treat to stop by Buscioni and pick up a soft, warm bun straight from the oven, filled with custard, chocolate, or marmalade, and topped with the usual dusting of granulated sugar for good measure. The other baked goods here look good, too, but everyone seems to come for the *bomboloni*.

Castaldini

Viale dei Mille 47r (Campo di Marte), 055/579-684
Open Wednesday through Monday 7:30 AM to 1:30 pm and 4:30 pm to
8:30 pm; closed most of August

Enzo Castaldini and his wife have been filling the community's need for cakes and cookies since 1956. If you do make it out this way, northeast of the center, you might want to take home the specialty of the house, the *torta Fernanda*, two layers of vanilla cake lightly soaked in liqueur, split in two, filled with whipped cream, and topped with powdered sugar and a little cocoa powder. The refrigerated case holds frozen cakes, profiteroles, and other goodies. During Carnival season, at the end of January and beginning of February, they also sell a fair number of *schiacciata alla*

Biscottini di Prato

The biscotti that are a favorite snack and dessert of Florence originate in the nearby town of **Prato**, about twenty minutes away by train. **Antonio Mattei** first opened his shop there in 1858, baking small, crescent-shaped almond cookies, and his company, now run by the Pandolfini family, is still the first name in biscotti (you'll sometimes see them called *cantucci* or *cantuccini*, but they are the same thing). Mattei also bakes other cookies, including *brutti ma buoni* (ugly but good), made with almonds, and *pan di ramerino*, another local favorite that combines raisins and rosemary in a sweet and savory bread that's great for breakfast.

You can find Mattei cookies for sale at most good wine and gourmet food shops in Florence, including **Gambi** and **Alessi** (page 53). The best way to avoid breaking a tooth when indulging in one of these twice-baked sweets is to immerse it in a small glass of *vin santo*, which is exactly what many Florentines do for dessert.

Antonio Mattei
Via Ricasoli 20–22, Prato, 0574/257-56; open Tuesday through Friday 8 AM to 8 PM, Saturday 8 AM to 1 PM and 3 PM to 7:30 PM, Sunday 8 AM to 1 PM.

fiorentina, a delicate yellow cake flavored with orange zest, topped with powdered sugar and the lily emblem of Florence etched in cocoa powder. You can also buy little chocolate candies, including chocolate-covered cherries and sugared oranges, and house-made butter cookies.

Minni ✻

Via Antonio Giacomini 16 (Piazza Savonarola), 055/578-836
**Open Monday through Saturday 7:15 AM to 8 PM, Sunday 7 AM to 1:30 PM;
closed August**

On the north side of Florence, wedged between Piazza Libertà and Piazza Savonarola, Minni is a great stop for a coffee and a pastry. It's also a smart choice for picking up cookies, cakes, and *semifreddi* to bring to a dinner party; Florentines will be impressed by your having discovered one of their finest pastry shops. Brioches in Florence tend to be of pretty decent quality, but Minni makes some of the freshest, best-tasting ones around, with raisins, filled with custard, and so on. In the refrigerated case, you'll find different sizes of *tartufi* and mounds of gelato covered in chocolate that look like little chocolate bombes. The staff is terrifically friendly and helpful.

Serafini

Via Gioberti 68r (Piazza Beccaria), 055/247-6214
Open Monday to Saturday 7:30 AM to 8 PM
Map J5

The glass case in this good-looking bar shows off an abundance of fresh pastries and sweets, while the busy bariste churn our top-flight cappuccinos and coffees all day. This is also a popular stop for a quick lunch (page 81).

GELATO

Gelateria L'Alpina

Viale Strozzi 12r (Fortezza da Basso), 055/496-677
Open Wednesday through Monday 7 AM to 9 PM in winter, 7 AM to midnight in summer; closed mid-August, Christmas Day, and New Year's Day

Like Cavini (see page 160), Alpina is a neighborhood hangout as well as gelato joint and bar. It's about a fifteen-minute walk from the train station, just by the Fortezza da Basso. The Buontalenti flavor is a bit disappointing (too much rum), but the chocolate, *nocciola* (hazelnut), and *croccante al rhum* are rich and creamy. On summer evenings, the sidewalk is filled with people of all ages slurping delicious cones.

Badiani ✳

Viale dei Mille 2or (Campo di Marte), 055/578-682
Open Wednesday through Monday 7 AM to midnight in winter, until 1 AM in summer

Badiani is the queen bee of Florentine gelaterias. You'll want to make a trip out to this inconvenient spot near the Campo di Marte for one reason: Buontalenti. Named after a late-sixteenth-century engineer and architect (designer of several Medici villas and the grotto in the Boboli Gardens), this is Badiani's signature flavor, and you'll notice that most customers regularly order it as part of their mélange of scoops. Buontalenti is the color of buttermilk and has no discernable flavor, like vanilla or some liqueur. Instead, it tastes like some kind of heart-stopping quadruple cream straight from the cow. It's decadent, delicious, and goes exceptionally well with Badiani's other flavors, hazelnut, coffee, and pistachio among them. Unlike most gelaterias, Badiani is also a pleasant bar where you can get a coffee and brioche and hang out with a book or newspaper. There's often a big rush after soccer matches at the nearby stadium.

Cavini
Piazza delle Cure 19-23r (Le Cure), 055/587-489
Open Tuesday through Sunday 7 AM to 1 AM

The draws here are the particularly wide variety of flavors and the generally high quality of the ice cream. As a bonus, once you have your cone or cup in hand, you can relax outside in one of the chairs on the piazza. Cavini's chocolate is rich and creamy, and there are variations on the theme: chocolate with orange, Mexican chocolate, and two kinds of chocolate chip, among others. It also has two varieties of pistachio (the Sicilian one is better), many fruit flavors, and an entire case of *semifreddi*, the half-frozen mousse counterpart to regular gelato. The Buontalenti flavor has a hint of saffron or some other mystery flavor that I like, though it's not quite as good as at Badiani (see page 159). Locals come by to pick up a frozen confection or *cassata* (Sicilian ricotta cake) to take home. Cavini also serves as a neighborhood hangout, staying open late to serve coffee, wine and spirits, and many, many cones of gelato.

Il Sorriso
Via Erbosa 70 (Gavinana), 055/689-007
Open Monday through Friday, noon to 11:30 PM, Saturday 11:30 AM to 11:30 PM, and Sunday 10:30 AM to 11:30 PM

This neighborhood gelato gem is in the Gavinana suburb, across from the gigantic Co-op supermarket and around the corner from La Piazzetta (page 152). Families with kids line up at night to get cones, cups, and cartons to go (the latter are unusual for Italy, because most gelato loses its luster within a day of being made). Il Sorriso is unremarkable looking and has fewer flavors than the bigger counterparts, like Vivoli and Badiani, but the gelato is first-rate and abundant. Try the *pinolo* (pine nut), coffee, or Buontalenti flavors. If you're in the mood for something fruitier, order the banana or strawberry. The portions are huge and affordable here compared to gelaterias in the Center.

MARKETS AND SHOPS

Cascine Market
Viale Lincoln, Parco delle Cascine
Open Tuesdays 8 AM to 2 PM, Sundays before Easter and Christmas Day 8 AM to 2 PM

It's a fun outing to come to the Cascine park on a Tuesday morning, stroll along the river, and check out the seemingly endless flea market here (it literally goes for several kilometers). The beginning is mostly food: good produce, cheeses, breads, and more. After that—and for most of the market—you will find stall after stall of cheap shoes, socks, bargain sleepwear and clothes, baby clothes, and more. You can find good deals here on simple cooking items like stainless-steel pots, strainers, and other little implements, and occasionally, attractive dishes at a good price. Steer clear of the *porchetta* stands even though they might look appealing. This isn't the place to sample the local specialties.

Pamela Sheldon Johns of Culinary Arts conducts a tasting of aged balsamic vinegars.

8
COOKING CLASSES

In a city that's as food-saturated as Florence, it's natural that the abundance would extend to cooking instruction, from one-day classes for beginners to semester-long courses complete with chefs' toques and test kitchens. Two different kinds of programs in and around Florence cater to the needs of food lovers seeking a Tuscan culinary education. The first type is geared toward residents or long-term visitors to the city. These schools offer both short- and long-term study, and professional (or at least semiprofessional) courses aimed at people interested in working within the restaurant industry. Then there is the large (and ever-growing) number of programs aimed at short-term vacationers, including some in which the cooking course *is* the vacation. It's not hard to see the appeal: what could be nicer than spending a week at a restored Tuscan villa, learning to cook traditional recipes with local ingredients?

IN FLORENCE

Apicius
Via Guelfa 85, 055/265-8135 or 055/265-6689
www.apicius.it
Map E2

This cooking school has refurbished its facilities to a high professional level. In the cooking classes, students stand at their own stainless-steel work station until the end of the semester, at which point they try out what they've learned in a fully stocked facsimile of a restaurant kitchen. The wine courses are held in a small classroom equipped with marble-topped desks containing little troughs for discarded wine.

Courses are divided into professional and amateur programs. The professional programs in the wine, cooking, and hospitality trades each last two semesters, at the end of which you receive a certificate of graduation (the school is private and not accredited by the state but is a member of the International Association of Culinary Professionals). You can also choose to enroll in just one semester. Each semester is a full load of Italian language, plus four subject courses and an internship at a restaurant or enoteca in Florence. The cost of a semester (approximately fifteen weeks) is $4,500 and also includes two knives and a jacket. The courses, which are all taught in English by Italian experts in the field, attract a mix of Americans and others from all over the world. Many are recent college graduates, while others are older professionals interested in changing careers.

The amateur programs are less intensive and can be taken either for a month, a week, a summer, or a semester. Subjects range from wine appreciation to regional cooking. You can also combine different subjects. Group amateur classes are sometimes taught in Italian, so make sure to check in advance. Or, sign up for one-on-one lessons in another one of the sparkling test kitchens. The school will help students find housing in Florence (not an easy thing) at fairly reasonable prices.

Cordon Bleu

Via di Mezzo 55r, tel./fax 055/234-5468
www.cordonbleu-it.com
Map G4

Cordon Bleu is run by Gabriella Mari and Cristina Blasi, two energetic Tuscan women with a vast knowledge of wine and food. They offer two different types of courses. The first is a week-long intensive course taught in English, on either basic Italian cooking, regional Italian cooking, or new Italian cooking. Each course is taught in four lessons of three hours each and costs €350. These classes are usually taught at intervals in April, June, July, and September, so you need to catch them at the right time in order to participate.

For the rest of the year, the school is aimed at residents and long-term visitors. It offers weekly courses, each with one to eight lessons, depending on the subject, and with each lesson running three hours. The best thing about these classes, and what sets them apart from the majority of cooking ventures in Florence, is that they are taught in Italian (often lightening-fast Italian) and, in addition to international students, attract a large number of Florentines, especially the night courses, which last from 8 to 11 PM. Some of the best classes are Primi Piatti, Cucina Mediterranea, and any of the vegetable classes.

One drawback here is that the kitchen design, which allows only one or two students at a time to participate hands-on, while the others sit, watch, and take notes. Another is that a lot of recipes are squeezed into each lesson, which can yield a hectic feel, but you do learn a lot of different techniques. A full-semester course includes all the classes offered. (New students should know that this school, Scuola Cucinaria di Cordon Bleu, is not related to the Cordon Bleu of Paris.)

Divina Cucina—Judy Witts Francini
Via Taddea 31, tel./fax 055/292-578
www.divinacucina.com
info@divinacucina.com
Map E2

Judy Witts Francini is a lively, outgoing cook with a thorough knowledge of Tuscan cooking. She earned her chops as a pastry chef for five-star hotels in San Francisco before moving to Italy in the 1980s and has worked in many Italian restaurants, including a *stage* with butcher Dario Cecchini. In 1988, she began teaching classes to small groups. She now offers lessons three days a week, generally from 10 AM to 4 or 5 PM, Tuesday through Thursday. Classes begin with a trip to the Central Market, literally across the street from her teaching kitchen. The day might include tastings of olive oils, balsamic vinegars, and local cheeses and finish with the cooking and eating of a full Tuscan meal. Students can come for just one class or up to three, as they choose; the cost is $375 for one day, $700 for two, and $1000 for a three-day course. Witts has also started doing tours and cooking classes in Chianti.

Judy Witts Francini and students in the Central Market.

Jeff Thickman
055/730-9064
www.jeffthickman.com
jig@dada.it

Jeff Thickman studied at the Cordon Bleu in Paris and has catered parties for the first families of Florence, as well as fashion and music royalty from around the world. He has also worked as the private chef to Zubin Mehta and at various times has cooked for Shimon Peres, Hillary Clinton, Sophia Loren, Luciano Pavarotti, Madonna, and Sting.

Thickman now divides his time between catering and teaching cooking classes at his home in Scandicci, outside Florence. He has outfitted the upstairs portion of his house as a complete teaching *laboratorio* for small group classes, where he can tailor the program to whatever his students would like to learn, from stretching pasta by hand to making Neapolitan *sfogliatelle* (flaky, ricotta-stuffed pastry). Classes are organized by request and have a minimum of four people and a maximum of twenty. Classes cost €140 per person. Whole-day extravaganzas, which include a tour of the Central Market, cost €250 per person.

Market to Table—Faith Willinger

Via della Chiesa 7, tel./fax 055/233-7014
www.faithwillinger.com
info@faithwillinger.com
Map C6

Faith Heller Willinger has lived in Florence for more than twenty-five years and has authored a cookbook on Italian vegetables (*Red, White & Greens*) and a guidebook on eating in northern Italy (*Eating in Italy*), and a new book that is part cookbook and part memoir called *Adventures of an Italian Food Lover.* Every Wednesday, she leads a small group on a tour of the local market and then cooks a full meal for her students while explaining what it is like to live and eat *alla italiana.* The classes start out with an introduction to real Italian coffee and work their way through olive oil, balsamic vinegar, wines of the region, and whatever Italian specialties she is cooking that day. Willinger, a down-to-earth woman with a great sense of humor, is well respected in both American and Italian food circles. Her Wednesday classes run $520 per person and include bottles of olive oil, vinegar, and other small gifts. You save $50 if you book directly through her Web site.

In addition, Willinger's colleague Jennifer Schwartz offers a food and wine tour of Florence to small groups. Schwartz, who has lived in Florence for more than a decade, takes visitors on a half-day city walk that includes tastings of coffee, olive oil, *salumi,* and more and finishes with a sit-down lunch. The cost is $260, including all food and wine.

Zibibbo—Benedetta Vitali

Via di Terzollina 3r (Careggi), tel. 055/433-383, fax 055/428-9070
www.zibibbonline.com
zibibbofirenze@hotmail.com
Map

Master chef and restaurateur Benedetta Vitali runs a small cooking school from her restaurant's kitchen (see Zibibbo, page 151), with courses geared toward people interested in working in a professional kitchen. For the five-day intensive lessons, Vitali and all the regular Zibibbo cooks take part in teaching the classes, which cover the basics of making *soffritto* (the base for savory Tuscan sauces) and stocks; frying vegetables, meats, and fish; cooking pasta and sauces; and making desserts from Zibibbo's recipe file. Courses go from 8 AM to 1 PM; the cost is €660 and includes wine tasting, an apron, and a hat but not lodging. They will also arrange one-day courses, which begin with a lesson and some work in the restaurant kitchen, and finish with lunch. These cost €140 including wine and food.

The school also offers a more relaxed curriculum aimed at Florentine residents. It is held over four Saturdays, during which students learn about pasta, cooking basics, and fish and at the end of each four-hour lesson make a complete meal. The cost is €385 and includes an apron and hat.

Outside Florence

Badia a Coltibuono

Gaiole (Chianti), tel. 0577/744-832, fax 0577/749-235
www.coltibuono.com
badia@coltibuono.com
See map on page 172

Badia a Coltibuono is one of the most scenic wineries in the Chianti region, an eleventh-century monastery overlooking the Val di Orcia near Gaiole in Chianti. Celebrated Italian cookbook author Lorenza de' Medici has retired, and cooking classes are now taught by her oldest son, Guido Stucchi. The courses, which are offered many times throughout the year, last six days and cost around €2,500, including accommodations. The course might include a day trip to Florence's Central Market and a visit to a nearby sheep farm, as well as extensive hands-on instruction in Tuscan cooking. The school also offers "mini classes" every Friday morning from 10 AM to 3 PM that include a visit to the cellars and a wine tasting. Call or write ahead to reserve for both kinds of classes.

Foods of Italy

U.S. tel. 646/638-0883; fax 646/638-0381
www.bugialli.com

Giuliano Bugialli is known for his numerous books on Tuscan and Italian regional cooking (*The Fine Art of Italian Cooking*, *Foods of Italy*), but even before he began writing cookbooks, he founded this cooking school to teach his craft to others.

In 1996, Bugialli opened a new location for his school in a restored farmhouse outside Florence in the Chianti region. Students stay in a hotel in Florence but are bused to the farmhouse for all classes. The school offers what it calls classic courses and traveling courses. The classic courses, which last one week, include Florence in the Spring, Italian Tradition, and Florence in the Fall. An example of the traveling courses is Umbria, Assisi, and Black Truffles. The cost of the classes is $3,600, including double room accommodation and some dinners.

Culinary Arts

U.S. tel. 805/963-7289; Italy tel. 0578/798-370
www.foodartisans.com
pamela@foodartisans.com
See map on page 172

Pamela Sheldon Johns, author of a popular series of single-subject cook-books, including *Parmigiano!* and *Balsamico!*, runs a cooking school in the countryside near Montepulciano. Students stay at Poggio Etrusco, Johns's restored fifteen-acre estate. Classes last one week and cost about $3000, including lodging for two, all food and wine, and ground transport. The workshops include visits to local farmers' and gourmet markets to highlight basic ingredients; wine tasting in nearby towns; visits to local Italian guest chefs; pizza making; and a farewell dinner at a memorable restaurant.

Toscana Saporita

U.S. tel. 212/219-8791, Italy tel. 0584/927-81
www.toscanasaporita.com
info@toscanasaporita.com

Anne Bianchi, author of several cookbooks, including *Italian Festival Food*, *Dolci Toscani*, and *From the Tables of Tuscan Women*, founded this cooking school with her Tuscan cousin, Sandra Lotti. The instructors include Lotti and several Americans (many Italian Americans), all experienced chefs and food professionals. Students come for one-week sessions to live and study in a fifteenth-century villa near Lucca. The classes are relatively small (twelve students maximum) and are taught in English. Emphasis is on hands-on participation and traditional Tuscan seasonal cooking. The price per person is $2,450, including double room accommodation, all food and wine, sightseeing tours, and pickup and drop off at the Pisa airport or train station. The cost is slightly higher for an advanced cooking course and a wine lover's course. There is a swimming pool and garden on the villa grounds and nearby hiking trails.

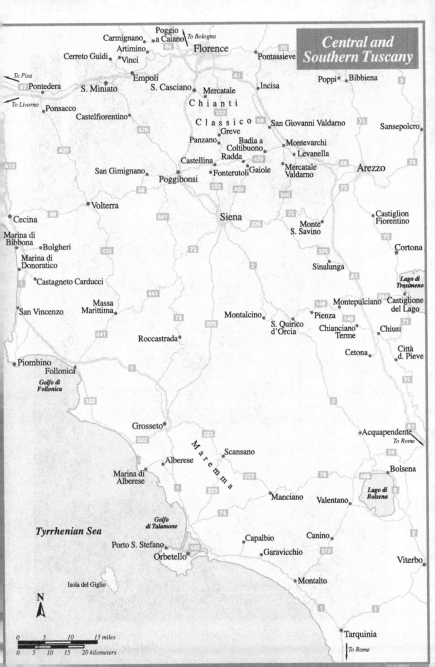

Central and Southern Tuscany

To Pisa
To Livorno
To Bologna

Carmignano
Poggio a Caiano
Artimino
Vinci
Cerreto Guidi
Florence
Pontassieve
Poppi
Bibbiena
Pontedera
Empoli
S. Miniato
S. Casciano
Mercatale
Incisa
Ponsacco
Castelfiorentino
Chianti
Panzano
Classico
Greve
San Giovanni Valdarno
Sansepolcro
Volterra
Badia a Coltibuono
Montevarchi
Levanella
Castellina
Radda
Mercatale Valdarno
Arezzo
San Gimignano
Fonterutoli
Gaiole
Poggibonsi
Cecina
Siena
Monte S. Savino
Castiglion Fiorentino
Marina di Bibbona
Bolgheri
Cortona
Marina di Donoratico
Lago di Trasimeno
Castagneto Carducci
Sinalunga
Massa Marittima
Montepulciano
Castiglione del Lago
San Vincenzo
Montalcino
Pienza
Chiusi
Roccastrada
S. Quirico d'Orcia
Chianciano Terme
Città d. Pieve
Piombino
Cetona
Follonica
Golfo di Follonica
Grosseto
Acquapendente
To Rome
Alberese
Scansano
Maremma
Bolsena
Marina di Alberese
Lago di Bolsena
Manciano
Valentano
Golfo di Talamone
Tyrrhenian Sea
Capalbio
Canino
Porto S. Stefano
Garavicchio
Orbetello
Viterbo
Isola del Giglio
Montalto
Tarquinia
To Rome

N

0 5 10 15 miles
0 5 10 15 20 kilometers

9

CULINARY EXCURSIONS
IN TUSCANY

If you want to taste the best that Tuscany has to offer, you will want to set out from Florence to explore the surrounding region. Some of the best restaurants can be found by the side of the road, in a small hilltop town, or seemingly in the middle of nowhere.

Tuscany covers a large swath of central Italy, bordered by the Apennines in the north, Umbria to the east, the region of Lazio straight south, and the Mediterranean Sea on the west. When you head toward Umbria, the cooking becomes more rustic, featuring wild game, heavy *ragù* sauces, and in season, prized black and white truffles. Along the coast you'll find excellent fish and shellfish, plus some specialty items like *cecina*, a fried savory snack made from chickpea flour. The rolling hills of Chianti, just south of Florence, offer not only a wealth of wine, but also a number of excellent country restaurants featuring simple Tuscan standards like braised wild boar and fresh *pici*.

In general, I'd much rather travel by train than car in Italy. I prefer to read, relax, and leave the driving to some nice man in a conductor's cap and leave the *autostrada* to the maniacs who want to see what their Fiat Punto can do when pushed to pass on a curve. Many of the destinations in this chapter can be reached by train or bus. However, I've come around to the reality that in order to see—and eat—the best of Tuscany, you need to have a car at least part of the time. With a car, you'll make short work of the curving country roads of Chianti, wandering from one winery to another. And you'll be able to reach that obscure enoteca or cheese shop that everyone's talking about without spending half your day looking mournfully into the distance for signs of the big, blue SITA bus. From Florence, you can hit the *autostrada* or a smaller, more scenic road and immediately you're in Greve, you're in Bolgheri, you're in Arezzo, trying out a little bit of what the rest of Tuscany has to offer.

This chapter delivers just a taste of Tuscany, with six personalized food-and-wine "itineraries" based on my own travels in the region. These excursions should be seen as both suggestions and inspiration for charting your own explorations. The itineraries are organized, more or less, starting with what is closest to Florence and then moving outward.

ITINERARY NUMBER 1:
DA DELFINA AND THE MEDICI VILLAS

If you have a car and a full day, you can visit three Medici villas, the town of Carmignano (home of great wines and a Pontormo masterpiece), and a fantastic country restaurant at the edge of an unreconstructed hill town, all within about forty minutes northwest of Florence.

Beginning in the mid-fifteenth century, the ruling Medici family established several country residences in the hills around Florence. Probably the most impressive to visit today is **Poggio a Caiano** (Piazza de' Medici 14, 055/877-012; open daily 9 AM to 4:30 pm, but the closing time changes frequently), well hidden behind a wall in the town of the same name (look out for a tiny placard reading *ingresso*). Once inside the courtyard, your first view is of a grand manicured lawn and the Renaissance palazzo, fronted by a dramatic curved double stairway and a Greek-style pediment (the first private home to incorporate one) with a terra-cotta frieze of mythological subjects. The inside is largely furnished, but not from Medici times. Victor Emmanuel II lived here for five years in the nineteenth century when Florence was briefly made the capital of Italy after unification. The most important room to see is the grand Sala di Leone X, which is covered with an impressive fresco cycle of Roman histories and mythological scenes painted by **Andrea del Sarto, Iacopo Pontormo**, and others between 1519 and 1521 and finished over half a century later (in a more mannerist style) by **Alessandro Allori**.

Next, head to the sleepy little town of **Carmignano**—better known as an excellent wine appellation—to see the stunning **Pontormo** altarpiece, *The Visitation*, in the church of San Michele. The painting (from the late

1520s) is of four women: Mary and Elizabeth, pregnant with Jesus and John the Baptist, respectively, and their older maidservants. Pontormo's vision of the visitation is an intimate and affectionate gathering, notable for the tranquil beauty of the faces (Mary and Elizabeth in profile, their maidservants directly facing the viewer), and the substantial figures draped in the vividly colored flowing garments for which the painter is well known. The women form a circle that seems to almost float in front of the obscure dark background of a narrow street in a quiet hill town.

Across from the small hill town of **Artimino**, the **Villa Medicea La Ferdinanda** (Viale Papa Giovanni XXIII 1, 055/875-1427) cuts a striking figure. This former hunting lodge, designed by **Bernardo Buontalenti**, is now a privately owned villa that can be rented for private and corporate functions. Although it is not open to visitors, you can wander the grounds and admire the building, with its jumble of chimneys, before eating at **Da Delfina** (page 176). Or, you can stay in the former stables, today a swanky inn called **Paggeria Medicea** (055/875-141) that is also home to a respected restaurant, **Biagio Pignatta** (055/875-1406; open Thursday 7:30 PM to 10:30 PM, Friday to Tuesday 12 PM to 2:30 PM and 7:30 PM to 10:30 PM). The villa produces a fine group of Carmignano wines under the Fattoria di Artimino label as well.

A view of the Medici villa from Artimino.

Chef-owner Carlo Cioni of Da Delfina.

Da Delfina
Via della Chiesa 1, Artimino, 055/871-8119
Open Tuesday through Saturday 12:30 pm to 3 pm and 8:30 pm to 10 pm,
Sunday 12:30 pm to 3 pm; closed August
€€-€€€

At the edge of Artimino sits a stone farmhouse with a large patio that overlooks a deep green valley across to the Medici villa on the other side. This is Da Delfina, a quintessential Tuscan country restaurant: scenic, rustic, regional . . . the real thing. (It also provided inspiration for the name and menu at the acclaimed restaurant Delfina in San Francisco.)

To start the meal, you are served a glass of local pink *spumante*, which complements starters like crostini of chicken liver and caramelized cherry tomatoes, a classic mixed *salumi* sampling, or an outstanding plate of bruschetta with fig spread and prosciutto. No matter how you feel about *ribollita*, you must try the version here: a thick stew that is then grilled, which brings out the flavor of the beans and *cavolo nero*. The fresh pasta dishes, such as *pappardelle* with rabbit *ragù*, are all terrific. For secondi, try the *fritto misto* of chicken, meat, and vegetables, each fried with a different batter; a veal scallopine; or any of the grilled or roasted meats. If the kitchen is frying zucchini flowers and/or artichokes, make sure to try those, too. If you order the succulent rabbit cooked with olives and pine nuts, no whistles or buzzers go off, but at the end of your meal you'll be given a special commemorative plate.

Even though Da Delfina has been written up in several guidebooks and magazines, it is usually filled with locals and regulars who have been coming to this family restaurant for years. The town is hard to find at the end of a very windy road. The extraordinary view and the hairy road make Delfina a better choice for lunch than dinner.

⸫ ⸫ ⸫

Continuing on the villa tour, a quick stop is all that's needed at the **Medici villa** in **Cerreto Guidi** (Via dei Ponti Medicei 7, 0571/557-07; open daily 8:30 AM to 6:30 pm; closed the second and third Monday of the month), also designed by **Buontalenti**. Not as grand or exciting as the other two villas, it is nonetheless the site of a grisly family murder: **Isabella de' Medici**, daughter of Duke Cosimo I, was strangled by her husband here in 1576. Today the bare villa, reached via an enormous double ramp in front, leads to a small but elegant trellised garden.

While in this area, you might want to stop in the nearby hill town of **Vinci** to see the small museum and birthplace of **Leonardo**, the town's most famous son. **Museo Leonardiano** is located in Palazzina Uzielli (Piazza Conti Guidi; open daily 9:30 AM to 7 pm); for more information call 0571/568-012. None of Leonardo's few works remain in Vinci, nor are the Vinci sights essential visiting for those strapped for time. It does, however, remain a lovely village, beautifully situated along the ridge of a hill above the small Streda River.

ITINERARY NUMBER 2:
SOLOCICCIA AND A FOOD AND
WINE TOUR OF CHIANTI

The green and hilly area between Florence and Siena could hardly be more beautiful. This is what people are thinking about when they get that faraway look in their eyes and wax poetic about the Tuscan countryside: mile after mile of undulating hillside vineyards and olive groves occasionally interrupted by a sixteenth-century farmhouse, and navigable by the kind of winding country roads that make people go out and buy expensive cars. The map of this unspoiled terrain reads like a local wine list: **Fonterutoli, Lamole, Olena, Querceto,** and on and on. In an agricultural area with such good wine, you are bound to find equally good food, and Chianti does not disappoint, with a bounty of welcoming country restaurants and famous butchers selling the Chianina beef and signature *salumi* of the area.

Until a dozen or so years ago, the concept of wine tourism was unknown here and seemed as odd to locals as someone asking to visit the cows on a farm. The wineries of Chianti have made dramatic leaps in allowing people to visit and taste the wares. Still, Chianti is no Napa, set up from top to bottom for tourists, and that's probably for the best. The drawback is that you will often arrive at a winery to find that the owners are having their lunch/are closed/are busy/don't do tastings/don't do tastings for small groups/don't do tastings on the first Saturday of the month/or simply don't like the look of you! This means that you are likely to spend a decent amount of time driving and enjoying the views without a lot of actual wine tasting and winery touring. To minimize wasted time, try to call in advance and make an appointment; otherwise, try to visit wineries on a weekday and in the morning, when many more of them are open. Some wineries will charge you for the tour and/or extensive tastings, but no matter where you are, the cost should not be high. Happily, many Chianti wineries sell their wines directly to customers at a slight discount.

Greve is the heart of the Chianti region and its biggest town, though still a small and tranquil place. The charmed, colonnaded triangle of

Piazza Matteotti at its center is home to four or five trattorias, a gelateria, and one of Tuscany's best butcher shops.

If you're hungry for lunch, stop at **Nerbone a Greve** (Piazza Matteotti 22, 055/853-308; €), owned by the same family that dishes out *bollito* sandwiches at Florence's Central Market and excellent Tuscan fare at Vecchia Bettola (see page 132). You can order a *bollito* at the bar or sit down and enjoy a hearty pasta with peas and sausage, a Tuscan peasant bean soup, or something lighter, like a chicken salad, all washed down with local wine.

Across the piazza, foodies from all over the world come to peruse the pork products at **Antica Macelleria Falorni** (Piazza Matteotti 69, 055/853-029, www.falorni.it; open Wednesday to Monday 12:30 PM to 10 PM), often credited with reintroducing Chianina beef into the Tuscan food scene. Several menacing stuffed *cinghiali* keep watch over the vast expanse of musky salami, cured meats, fresh meats, and cheeses. Here you'll find every variation of salami, made from pork, boar, and the special pig called Cinta Senese (see page 26). The shop also stocks vacuum-packed prosciutto and *bresaola* and sells fresh Chianina beef, milk-fed veal, and local chickens.

If you would like to see (or sample) the full gamut of Chianti's viticultural output, plan a stop at **Le Cantine di Greve** in Chianti (Piazza delle Cantine 2, just after the footbridge into town, 055/854-6404, www.lecantine.it; open daily 10 AM to 7 PM). It boasts the biggest selection of wines in Chianti, plus a nice assortment of extra virgin oils, *vin santo*, and other local goods.

On the third weekend of September, the towns of Greve and Panzano hold a joint wine festival called **Vino al Vino**, with festivities taking place in both towns. For more information, call the Greve tourism office, 055/854-51.

Driving south from Florence into Greve, you'll pass the **Castello di Verrazzano** winery (Route 222, right side of road traveling south, 055/854-243, www.verrazzano.com; closed December and January; guided visits of the winery are offered Monday to Friday at 10 and 11 AM). You can stop for a tasting of Chianti Classico, *vin santo*, olive oil, or honey at the winery's roadside store, or, if you're there at the right time, you can explore the castle and wine cellars.

Less accessible but worth the detour is the **Castello di Querceto** winery (Via Dudda, on the road between Greve and Dudda, 055/859-21, www.castellodiquerceto.it; open Monday to Friday 9 AM to 6 PM, Saturday afternoon in spring and summer), makers of highly respected Chianti Classico vintages. The castle and idyllic grounds (complete with strolling peacocks) are set in isolated splendor on top of a hill, next to acres of sloping vines. Call in advance to set up a tasting, or better yet, stay in one of their *agriturismo* apartments for a night or two.

A short drive south from Greve will put you in the small town of **Panzano**. This pleasant community harbors a couple of fine *enoteche* selling the wines of the region, but its claim to fame is **Antica Macelleria Cecchini** (Via XX Luglio 11, 055/852-020; open Monday through Tuesday and Thursday 9 AM to 2 PM, Saturday and Sunday 9 AM to 6 PM). This restored old-fashioned butcher shop, with a crowd always spilling onto the sidewalk, is presided over by **Dario Cecchini**, beaming like a bull in a red neck bandana behind his pristine meat case. This is a man who loves meat. He comes from a long line of Tuscan butchers, and his shop is the sanctum sanctorum of the cow. Cecchini has a flair for the dramatic: he likes to quote Dante at length and rhapsodize about famous friends and acquaintances around the world. His cultivated image as celebrity butcher would ring hollow, however, if he didn't back it up with such extraordinary products. While classical music wafts through his shop, you can help yourself to tastes of his incredible *porchetta, finocchiona* salami, and Parmesan dipped in his signature sweet-and-spicy pepper jelly. No, that fluffy white mountain inside the case isn't mashed potatoes, it's lard—or as one German tourist indicated to me with a sly smile, *schmaltz*. And you can taste that as well, spiked with herbs and spread on little toasts. Of course, you can also buy pork, lamb, and a huge selection of beef cuts, all overseen by Cecchini more or less from cradle to case.

Solociccia

Via Chiantigiana 5 (entrance on Via XX Luglio), 055/852-727
Open Thursday through Saturday 7 PM to 9 PM and 9 PM to 11 PM (two seatings), and Sunday lunch

€€

I am happy to report that fame has not spoiled **Dario Cecchini**. After gaining even more notoriety as the Tuscan butcher who teaches Bill Buford the ways of the cow in Buford's best-selling book *Heat*, Cecchini has opened a small, unusual restaurant across from his shop. You sit at communal tables in an old farmhouse that has been redone in a contemporary style, rubbing shoulders with a mix of Italians and foreigners, and eat homey, delicious food from a fixed menu: five-plus courses of meat—just meat. Well, what did you expect from a butcher?

The menu changes weekly but may include such starters as fried meatballs, crostini topped with ground beef and soaked in a tomatoey broth (so-called Christmas style), or tiny balls of lamb tartare impaled on a rosemary stem. A beautiful *pinzimonio*, a mix of raw vegetables for dipping in olive oil, acts as both an appetizer and a side dish for eating any time during the meal when you want a break from the meats. Everything is served family style, and there is plenty of food to go around. No primi are offered; instead a series of increasingly delicious meat dishes, almost all of them beef, come out of the kitchen one at a time: a simple sliced roast beef; tender chunks of "muscle" (*tenerumi*) served with a tangy *salsa verde*; beef scaloppine sauced with sweet tomatoes; and finally, a rich *stracotto chiantigiano* (beef braised in Chianti wine). Simple white beans are also passed around, along with Tuscan bread, house wine, and water. If you like, you can bring your own bottle of wine (no corkage fee), which I recommend. The house wine is just so-so, and a bottle of Chianti Classico from the enoteca down the street is a more fitting complement to the fantastic meat dishes. The cost per person is just thirty euros, including a cup of fine Piansa coffee and a slice of moist homemade yellow cake for dessert, followed by an assortment of mind-altering *digestivi* jovially passed around the table. (If you have a good group, by this time, you and your tablemates will all be on a first-name basis, clinking glasses and exchanging cheers in several languages.)

Although Solociccia opened in late summer 2006, it hit its stride immediately. I ate there in its second month and found it one of the most fun and unique dining experiences I've had in Italy. I know it won't be long before I have to call months in advance to get a reservation. In the meantime, I am going to make the hour-long drive from Florence as often as I can.

᠁ ᠁ ᠁

Continuing on the main road south from Panzano, keep an eye out on the left-hand side for a small sign reading **Tenuta Fontodi** (Via San Leonino 87, 055/852-005, www.fontodi.com; open daily 8 AM to 12:30 PM and 2 PM to 6 PM). Fontodi is one of the stars of the Chianti region; its Chianti Classicos and more expensive all-Sangiovese Flaccianello della Pieve consistently receive high praise. You'll find a small tasting room where you can sample some of the Chiantis, perhaps a white wine, and the winery's excellent olive oil and *vin santo*. Fontodi also offers lovely accommodations on the estate, a great option among *agriturismi* in the area.

Beyond Panzano, the road eventually splits and you have a choice of heading east toward Radda or west to Castellina. **Castellina** is the more charming and slightly bigger of the two, a thoroughly medieval village filled with wine shops and bars. It's a nice place simply to walk around and stop in at **La Bottega del Vino di Cantina Orlandi** (Via della Rocca, 13, 0577/741-110; open daily 10 AM to 1 PM and 4 PM to 7:30 PM). You'll find some of the big names of the Chianti and Montepulciano regions (**Castello di Ama, Felsina**), as well as many of the smaller producers from the hills right around Castellina. The selection is small but well chosen; I like to stop here to chat with Franco, the northern Italian who manages the place (he speaks fluent English and German) and to taste the various wines of the day.

About ten minutes south of Castellina you'll come across the tiny town of Fonterutoli, where if you blink you'll miss the turn-off for the winery and restaurant of the same name. Like Fontodi, **Fonterutoli** (Via Ottone III di Sassonia 5, 0577/741-385, finfo@enotecadifonterutoli.it; open for tastings by appointment) is another star of the region, consistently winning the coveted Tre Bicchieri (Three Glasses) award from

Gambero Rosso for their wine called Siepi, a mixture of Sangiovese and Merlot. Its Chianti Classico and Poggio alla Badiola are also highly praised. You can buy bottles in the winery's small store or eat a simple Tuscan meal at its unpretentious trattoria on the same road.

If you drive toward the tiny market town of **Gaiole in Chianti**, you'll pass Coltibuono. Follow the signs to **Badia a Coltibuono** (Loc. Badia a Coltibuono, 0577/ 744-81, www.coltibuono.com, info@coltibuono.com; shop open Monday 2 PM to 6:30 PM, Tuesday to Saturday 9:30 AM to 1 PM and 2 PM to 6:30 PM; closed mid-January to the end of February. Private winery tours by appointment), a former abbey that's now a winery best known for its reliable Chianti Classico. The casual and elegant restaurant and wine bar have been tastefully redone and occupy an unbeatable setting overlooking the surrounding green hillsides. A glass of wine here or a meal outdoors is to sample the Tuscan good life. Guided tours of the wine cellar and abbey are offered in the afternoons, from May to October. Call ahead to arrange wine or olive oil tastings (for groups of ten or more), or for cooking classes (see page 169).

ITINERARY NUMBER 3:
LA FRATERIA, MONTALCINO, MONTEPULCIANO, AND PIENZA

Back when the term *Supertuscan* had not yet been coined and Chianti was served in bulging straw-covered flasks, the winemakers south of Siena had a head start on the rest of Tuscany because of their tradition of high-quality—instead of just quantity—barrel-aged Brunello di Montalcino and Nobile di Montepulciano. And with the general tide that raised all boats in the 1980s, these wines, led by makers such as **Avignonesi** in Montepulciano and **Col d'Orcia** in Montalcino, became even better.

As in the Chianti region just to the north, where there's good wine, there's good food. Many of the area's wineries also serve hearty rustic meals in farmhouse settings to complement their full-bodied wines; and nearby **Pienza**, a pristine fifteenth-century hill town, is known for its excellent cave-aged pecorino cheeses. This area is what Tuscan dreams are made of, blanketed with vines and olive trees growing on sloping sunlit hillsides. In this same region, in the hills just east of the town of **Cetona**, is a thirteenth-century Franciscan monastery that has been transformed into a sanctuary of extraordinary food and spiritual rehabilitation.

Montalcino

If you are coming south from Florence or Siena, head first to Montalcino, a pleasant if not altogether arresting hill town, built fortress-style for strategic purposes in the days when catapulting boiling oil on your enemies was a serious option. Nowadays, the residents have far better uses for oil.

Just outside of town you'll find **Fattoria dei Barbi** (Loc. Podernuovi 170, 0577/848-277, www.fattoriadeibarbi.it), a full-service winery in every sense. You can eat lunch or dinner at its excellent restaurant, which features the outstanding Barbi *salumi*; *pici*, a local pasta specialty; and plenty of wild game. Of course, this kind of hearty food goes especially well with a bottle of Barbi Brunello. When you're done, take a tour of the wine cellars where the Brunello is aged in both French oak *barriques* and the bigger Slavic barrels. Selected tastings are also available, and you can buy the wines in the winery shop. In addition, there are a few apartments for rent by the week. The tasting room and tours last from 10 AM to 1 PM and 2:30 PM to 6 PM.

While in the area, stop in and visit other makers of fine Brunello, such as **Biondi-Santi** (Via Panfilo d'Oca, Montalcino, 0577/848-087, www.biondisanti.it). Tours of the cantina and tastings of its wines are by appointment only, but it's worth the trouble for the serious Brunello lover. **Col d'Orcia** (Sant'Angelo in Colle, just outside Montalcino, tel. 0577/808-091, fax 0577/844-018, www.coldorcia.it, info@coldorcia.it), famous for its fine Brunello, welcomes visitors for tastings at the on-site store, which is open Monday through Saturday 8:30 AM to 10:30 AM and 2:30 PM to 6 PM. More extensive tastings, and tours of the grounds and cellars, are done by appointment.

Pienza

About halfway between the two wine capitals of Montalcino and Montepulciano is Pienza, a town that looks frozen in time. Pienza was conceived and built in the fifteenth century under the direction of Pope Pius II, who hailed from the small town of Corsignano that already stood in the same spot. An immodest pontiff (he renamed the town after himself), but possessing good taste, he engaged architect **Bernando Rossellino**, a contemporary of Leon Battista Alberti, to oversee the building of stately Renaissance palazzi and piazzas. You can step into the Duomo, take a good look around the **Palazzo Piccolomini** next door, and stop to marvel at the geometric equilibrium achieved in this piazza, a model for many future Renaissance projects.

Aside from its architecture, Pienza is known for one thing: pecorino cheese. Pienza and the hills around it are the center of quality pecorino production in Tuscany, and all through the town and along the highways you'll see wheels of the pungent cheese for sale. Pecorino di Pienza is a cheese made of sheep's milk—usually pasteurized—shaped in smallish rounds and aged for varying amounts of time to create a range of cheeses from fresh and light to hard and tart. The outer rind is sometimes covered in a dried tomato paste or ash, but this doesn't affect the flavor. Pecorino goes well with pears and green apples. I also like to eat aged pecorino with a tangy *mostarda* (spicy chutney) or other sweet-spicy sauce, plus it pairs nicely with the local full-bodied red wines. You will find delicious cheeses to buy in both Pienza, at the shops lining the main street, and directly from the farmers in the surrounding hills.

Not far from Pienza, close to the slightly bigger towns of Trequanda and Sinalunga, is **Montisi**, a village so small it's not even marked on most maps. But in Italy one-horse towns often house two-star restaurants. **La Romita** (Via Umberto I 144, Montisi, tel. 0577/845-186, fax 0577/845-201, www.laromita.it, €€€) is not actually a Michelin-star restaurant, but the kitchen is cooking sophisticated meals worthy of acclaim far beyond this tiny community. If you can, sit outside on the *terrazza* overlooking a typically stunning Tuscan valley. The interior is also pleasant, decorated with frescoes and an odd assortment of bric-a-brac. You can order either à la carte or from a choice of tasting menus. The menu

Visitors strolling through the arched gates of Pienza.

leggero (light menu) consists of an antipasto, three small primi, and a dessert, while the menu *di campagna* (country menu) includes an antipasto, three primi, and two secondi, plus dessert if you have room for it. The antipasto is a large plate of unusual crostini, colorfully presented and topped with tomatoes, cheeses, *salumi*, liver pâté, onions, and lots of local olive oil. The kitchen focuses on old Tuscan dishes that have been largely forgotten, making use of porcini and other delicacies. Secondi are primarily grilled and roasted meats scented with rosemary and thyme. The wine list is heavy on the old-school Tuscan labels, staying consistent with the theme. Service is extremely sober and solicitous; the owner is likely also to be your waiter. In addition to the superb kitchen, La Romita is a comfortable place to spend the night and enjoy the idyllic swimming pool.

Montepulciano

In and around Montepulciano, you can easily get your fill of Nobile di Montepulciano, second only to Brunello in this part of the world. Nobile is made with a slight variation of the Sangiovese variety used in Brunello, but it contains a small percentage of other varietals and is not aged as long as Brunello, which usually means it's somewhat more affordable. The streets of the disarmingly pretty medieval hill town of Montepulciano practically flow red with wine, with plenty of little shops and *cantinette* offering the chance to taste and buy.

While in the region, stop in at **Poliziano** (Loc. Montepulciano Stazione, Via Fontago 1, 0578/738-171, Az.agr.poliziano@iol.it), which is owned by Federico Carletti and makes several refined Nobiles, as well as a Rosso and a Morellino di Scansano. Most of the wines are aged in small French oak barrels, giving them an elegant finish. You can tour the winery from 8:30 AM to 12:30 PM and 2:30 PM to 6:30 PM, except for Saturday and Sunday mornings. The winery also runs **Caffè Poliziano** (Via Voltaio del Corso 27, 0578/758-615; open daily 7 AM to midnight) in the center of town, where you can get a light bite to eat or a glass of one of its excellent wines.

La Frateria di Padre Eligio

One of the most unforgettable dining experiences in the area is the outstanding eight-course tasting menu at La Frateria, high in the leafy hills near Montepulciano. La Frateria is in no way an ordinary restaurant. For one, it is housed in an elegantly refurbished thirteenth-century Franciscan monastery. Adding to the surreal experience, most of the food, from the vegetables to the meat, is grown or raised on the restaurant's extensive grounds. La Frateria is part of Mondo X, a foundation established by Padre Eligio, a charismatic Catholic priest that helps young men recover from drug and alcohol addiction. As part of their recovery, the men work and live here (and at other locations around Italy), including in the kitchen and dining room.

La Frateria di Padre Eligio

Convento St. Francesco, Cetona, tel. 0578/238-261, fax 0578/239-220
frateria@ftbcc.it
www.mondox.it or www.lafrateria.it
Open Wednesday through Monday 1 PM to 3 PM and 8 PM to 10 PM
€€€€

Although officially La Frateria bears no Michelin stars, it is certainly on the level of the best restaurants in Italy in terms of food and service and surpasses most of them in atmosphere and history. The elegant dining room, softened by fresh flowers and linens, is built into the old stones of the monastery, allegedly founded by Saint Francis himself. The staff is made up of members of the Mondo X community, all immaculately groomed young men who lead you to your table and proceed to serve the food and wine with care and attention. The star here, however, is chef Walter Tripoli, who has studied with master chefs in Piedmont and Paris but seems to feel most at home with Tuscan traditions taken to a higher plane. The dishes on his tasting menu show a sophistication rarely seen in Florence but maintain the rustic flavor and flourish that distinguishes the unfussy cooking of this region.

Much of the fare—including the *spumante* served as an *aperitivo*, most of the vegetables, and even the meats—is made from ingredients grown and raised by the Mondo X communities. The meal begins with *spumante* and a platter of outstanding salami and prosciutto. The first few dishes are small and artfully presented, often with fish or poultry, and best accompanied with a white wine, such as a Greco di Tufo from Campania. Antipasti and primi might include a delicate whole smoked trout; a terrine of rabbit, prunes, and pine nuts that marries savory and sweet; and a more assertive orzo timbale with capers and green sauce.

The next dishes are slightly heavier, such as wild boar ravioli in a smoked duck sauce in which the ravioli are delicately striped like the Duomo of Siena. The secondo might consist of a tender, seared fillet of beef in a light peppercorn sauce. Desserts are mercifully light here. If you still have room, you'll be able to enjoy the lemon sorbet with strawberry sauce or a similar confection, followed by a selection of excellent and original little cookies, each one different from the others.

A meal here runs around eighty euros per person. The wine list is reasonable, offering an excellent range of choices from under twenty-five euros a bottle on up to a few times that for some of the best vintages of the region. The considerable cost of dining here is not surprising, however, given that this is a complete experience that cannot be compared to eating at a fancy eatery in the city center. Either before or after your meal, ask to be taken on a tour of the monastery grounds and the cantina where the wines are kept. A few one-time monks' cells have been refurbished for guests; the rooms cost just under two hundred euros per night.

ITINERARY NUMBER 4:
LA RENDOLA AND OUTLET SHOPPING
IN THE VALDARNO

About thirty miles southeast of Florence, a gaggle of tour buses gathers outside a long, low modern building amid the industrial clutter and green hillsides of the Valdarno area. Taxis pour out a rush of avid visitors; rental cars and even people on foot gather around the guarded entrance. If it's a weekend, you'll probably have to take a number and wait for ten or fifteen minutes while chatting with other eager attendees. What is this mysterious structure? A modern art museum? A repository of Tuscan treasures from Giotto to Vasari? Not at all. This is the Prada outlet, attracting fashion-conscious travelers from Kyoto to Toronto.

The small villages along the valley with their factories and industrial detritus have spawned a new kind of tourism in Italy. People now plan a trip to Prada, Gucci, and Dolce & Gabbana along with visits to the *David* and the Uffizi. Prices at these factory outlets are usually about 50 percent off retail, though you can find even deeper discounts on certain items, especially at the very end of a season. I've seen women and men walk out with half a dozen bags overflowing with shoes, purses, and all kinds of other booty.

The **Prada outlet**, also called **Space** or **I Pellettieri d'Italia** (Route 69, 055/919-6528), stands just past the town of Montevarchi, in a suburb called Levanella. It is unmarked and thus difficult to find, so once you're in Levanella, keep watch for a long, low white building on your left. It's likely you'll drive by it the first time, but don't worry: gas station attendants and *bariste* all over the area are used to pointing people in the right direction. The outlet is open Monday through Saturday 9:30 AM to 7:30 PM, Sunday 2 PM to 7:30 PM. In addition to the flagship Prada label, the outlet sells designs by Miu Miu, Helmut Lang, and Jil Sander. There is a café next door for coffee breaks and bored spouses.

The other outlets are all in different towns right off the A1 Autostrada. The **Dolce & Gabbana factory outlet** (Loc. S. Maria Maddalena, 49 Pian dell'Isola, Incisa, 055/833-1300; open Monday through Saturday 9 AM to 7 PM) is said to offer excellent deals, especially for men's clothing. You can also hit **The Mall** (Via Europa 8, 055/865-7775; open Monday through Saturday 10 AM to 7 PM, Sunday 3 PM to 7 PM) in Leccio Regello, which has outlets for Gucci, Giorgio Armani, Bottega Veneta, and Yves Saint Laurent.

Getting away from the fashion world, the designer glass manufacturer **IVV** has a factory store in the same vicinity (Lungarno Guido Reni 60, 055/944-444; open Monday through Saturday 9 AM to 1 PM and 4 PM to 8 PM; closed Monday morning) in San Giovanni Valdarno. Unfortunately, you won't find deep discounts on its selection of both elegant and more casual vases, Champagne glasses, and glass serving dishes, though it does have a larger selection than stores in Florence offering its wares, and it also has discounts on selected end-of-season items.

Osteria di Rendola

Via di Rendola 89, in the hills between Montevarchi and Mercatale Valdarno, 055/970-7491

Open Friday to Tuesday 12:30 PM to 2:30 PM and 7:30 PM to 10:30 PM, Thursday 7:30 PM to 10:30 PM

€€€

At Osteria di Rendola, set in the hills above Montevarchi, chef Alessandro Bettini serves updated Tuscan cuisine in a restored farmhouse. Some of his specialties include the classics, such as *ribollita* made with *zolfini* beans, *bistecca*, and *brasato*, and many more unusual dishes, including duck breast stuffed with olives on a plate of chickpea puree and sliced fennel. The wine list covers all of Italy, with an emphasis on reds and whites of Tuscany. La Rendola is also an *agriturismo* (country inn).

ITINERARY NUMBER 5:
DA VENTURA, WHITE TRUFFLES, AND THE PIERO TRAIL IN EASTERN TUSCANY

Around Florence and Rome, you'll sometimes hear travelers talking about following the Piero Trail. **Piero della Francesca** was one of the finest painters of the fifteenth century, his work a kind of prelude to the coming sophistication of depth, color, and delicate features of Leonardo da Vinci. Part of Piero's allure is that so few of his works remain and you must travel to see them, as they are concentrated in a corner of eastern Tuscany and western Umbria. This book is about food, but there's nothing wrong with picking up a little culture before or after a meal—this is Italy, after all. One of my favorite restaurants, Da Ventura, happens to be in Sansepolcro, the birthplace of Piero and home to some of his finest works.

Visitors do not need a car to reach **Arezzo**; it is easily reached by train and bus. **Sansepolcro** is best reached by car, and it is almost a two-hour drive from Florence on the A1 autostrada. I would recommend spending the night at one of the nice hotels, bed and breakfasts, or beautiful *agriturismi* in this area to make the most of this itinerary.

Truffles in Tuscany

For most people, prized black and white truffles bring to mind either central France's Périgord or northwest Italy, especially Alba and Asti in Piedmont. But Tuscany and Umbria are also notable centers of *tartufi*. In mid- to late November, a number of lively fairs and markets are held that celebrate the earthy *funghi*, which can sell for up to four thousand euros per kilogram. In and around the small town of San Miniato, just outside of Florence, and around the Umbrian towns of Norcia and Città di Castello, the truffle trade is particularly active. In restaurants, including the superb **Da Ventura** in Sansepolcro (see below), waiters use a custom instrument called a *tagliatartufi* (truffle slicer) to shave thin slices onto tagliatelle or ravioli, while signs posted by individuals along country roads announce truffles for sale by the *etto* (100 grams). To find out about the truffle market in **San Miniato,** where you can taste truffles and buy them fresh or as truffle oil, visit the town's website, www.comune.san-miniato.pi.it.

Da Ventura ✻

Via Aggiunti 30, Sansepolcro, 0575/742-560
Open Tuesday through Saturday 12:30 PM to 2:15 PM and 7:30 PM to 10:30 PM,
Sunday 12:30 PM to 2 PM; closed most of August and Christmas Day
€€

The first time I ate at Da Ventura, the experience left such an indelible impression on my gustatory memory that I was set on returning, which I have done every year or so since. Most meals would suffer under these conditions of fantasy and memory, but Da Ventura just seems to get better and better.

The atmosphere is simple and unassuming, with tablecloths and fine drinking glasses the only nods toward elegance; caricatures of Italian celebrities line the wood-paneled walls.

One image that lingered in my memory from the first visit was of big platters of *porchetta* (herbed pork cooked on a spit) and pasta with truffles served family-style from a rolling cart, and the cart still plays an important part in a meal here. The waiter will roll the antipasto cart over to the table and offer diners a taste of a dozen cold savory dishes, including prosciutto, stuffed eggplant, goat cheese, and anchovies. Pastas are served hot from the pan. In November and December, the restaurant boasts fresh *agnolotti* and ravioli served with butter and sage or fresh shaved white truffle, in addition to other tempting pastas. Whole roasts are then rolled out hot from the kitchen on their own cart and sliced for secondi. All of the meats are very appetizing; luckily, they offer a *tris* or tasting of all three: often *porchetta, stinco di vitello* (veal roast), and *stracotta* (wine-braised pot roast), each more delicious than the last. There is also a dessert cart, filled with housemade torts and custards, though I'll be impressed if you still have room. Finally, they make an excellent coffee at the little bar off the dining room.

This is one of my favorite places in Tuscany—it feels like an upscale country inn but is located in the middle of a historic town. And the cost is the same as a second-rate trattoria in Florence. The wine list is full of well-priced bottles, including several choices of Nobile di Montepulciano and Umbrian wines. Da Ventura can accommodate big groups with its many long tables; however, as always, be sure to reserve in advance.

■ ■ ■

Sansepolcro is a small, genteel town where you can happily pass a day. Aside from Da Ventura, its claim to fame is its **Museo Civico** (Via Aggiunti 65, 0575/732-218; open daily 9:30 AM to 1:30 PM and 2:30 PM to 6:30 PM), home to two of **Piero della Francesca's** best-known paintings. The museum houses the *Madonna della Misericordia*, which depicts members of the patrons' confraternity gathered under the Virgin's outspread cloak; and the *Resurrection*, painted in fresco for the nearby town hall in the 1450s and later detached and moved to the present site.

In the nearby town of **Arezzo**, Piero's masterwork, a fresco cycle depicting the *Legend of the True Cross* (*Legenda della Vera Croce*), was under restoration and out of public view for nearly a decade. Fortunately, it is now back on glorious display in the church of **San Francesco**.

To see the frescoes, you must first make an appointment by calling the Centro Prenotazione (0575/240-01); you then pick up your ticket at the office next to the church in the Piazza San Francesco. Visitors are restricted to fifteen-minute viewings. Pick up an audio guide (gratis) and let the gazing begin. When you're done, head across the street to refuel with a coffee or *aperitivo* at the Viennese-style **Caffè dei Costanti** (Piazza San Francesco 19).

Arezzo has had its brushes with fame: Piero's fresco cycle (a copy of it) was featured in the film *The English Patient*, and Roberto Benigni walked the streets of this, his hometown, in the movie *Life Is Beautiful*. The poet Petrarch and the sixteenth-century painter, architect, and historian Giorgio Vasari were born here, both still constant sources of pride to the local population. Arezzo is truly the epitome of an aesthetically pleasing and comfortably bourgeois Tuscan town. It is also a major antiques center, and every first Saturday and Sunday of the month an outdoor fair takes over half the city.

Those who are dedicated in their quest for a comprehensive Piero tour will drive to the nearby tiny town of **Monterchi** just to see his strikingly unusual *Madonna del Parto*. The work, which was originally in the town church, is now on display in a darkened, temperature-controlled room on Via Reglia. (Contradictory signs might have you going in circles, but don't worry, the town is so small you're bound to wind up here.) This painting is important as one of the only depictions of Mary as a pregnant woman, without the conventions of a Visitation scene. The fresco is worse for wear, but the beatific look on Mary's face transcends the passage of time.

Follow That Food Fair

Throughout the year, but especially in the warmer months, you'll begin to see brightly colored posters around Florence announcing *sagre* of various kinds, food fairs celebrating the local cuisines of Tuscany. You'll find everything from the Sagra del Cinghiale (Festival of the Wild Boar) and the Sagra del Fungo Porcino (Festival of the Porcini Mushroom) to *sagre* for fried pork chops, handmade pasta, white beans, and more. These fairs are usually in small towns on the outskirts of Florence that are difficult to reach without a car. Once you arrive, the *sagre* are just as much fun as you would imagine: casual, whole-hog celebrations of food with booths of different producers and purveyors offering their wares. Sometimes you pay a small entrance fee and other times you only pay for what you eat.

The exact dates and locations of the *sagre* change from year to year, so watch for the posters. For more information, contact the Tuscany tourism office at Via di Novoli 26, tel. 055/438-2111, fax 055/438-3084.

Sagra della Frittella (fritter)
Sambuca di Tavernelle Val di Pesa
Mid-May

Sagra dei Tortelli (potato-stuffed ravioli)
Scarperia
End of August

Sagra delle Pappardelle
Montespetoli
End of August, beginning of September

Mercato del Tartufo (truffle)
San Miniato
Mid-November

ITINERARY NUMBER 6:
GAMBERO ROSSO, GREAT WINE, AND FINE
BEACHES IN BOLGHERI AND THE MAREMMA

You could say that Sassicaia started it all. In the late 1960s, the Marchese Mario Incisa della Rocchetta decided it would be nice to grow some imported French grapes and experiment with making a new kind of Tuscan wine at his **Tenuta San Guido** estate in Bolgheri. A world-class wine was born—Sassicaia—and a quiet renaissance in the area was under way.

This southwest portion of Tuscany, called the Maremma, centered around the unsensational town of Grosseto, has traditionally been a low-profile spot. Until recently, you could barely find a paragraph on the area in most English guidebooks. Tuscans come here to hunt wild boar in winter, and the seaside—most of it developed in the nondescript contemporary Italian style—is frequented all summer by vacationing Italian families and visiting Germans. (In fact, many signs in the region are written in Italian and German.)

This sleepy region is starting to wake up, however. In the past fifteen years, the area has become a mecca for serious winemakers who want a piece of the Bolgheri *terroir*. It seems that the superior quality of the Maremma soil and the proximity to sea air have an especially positive effect on grapes. The names that made Bolgheri famous include **Tenuta San Guido, Ornellaia,** and **Guado al Tasso,** but in the late 1990s, it seemed as if every winemaker who had the *soldi* was buying up land in the area. Emerging producers such as Enrico Santini and Michele Satta are also turning out great product and getting better every year.

In addition to its world-class wineries, the area has several points of interest, especially for the intrepid food lover. **Alain Ducasse** has opened a deluxe hotel and restaurant in the neighborhood, close to Castiglione delle Pescaia. The unassuming port town of **San Vincenzo** offers a Michelin two-star eating experience by the sea and a fun and funky casual seafood spot just down the road. And about an hour south of San Vicenzo, in **Alberese,** you can find a lovely protected nature area and Tuscany's most beautiful beach, Marina di Alberese, complete with white sands and turquoise waters, but without the chaos and endless rows of *ombrelloni* found at most Italian beaches.

Visiting the Wineries

Wine tourism is a recently introduced concept for Tuscany, especially for this area, which hasn't had as much time as Chianti and Montalcino to get used to the idea. But with the biggest names in wine overrunning the region, it was only a matter of time before the marketing consultants from the Napa Valley and the Champagne region were brought in.

If you simply show up in the Bolgheri region, excited about the prospect of visiting the home of your favorite wines, you are bound to be disappointed. Instead of a slew of open tasting rooms, you'll find a series of barely marked villas sealed off to the drive-up visitor. However, you can still taste and buy the best local wines at **Enoteca Il Borgo** (Via Vittorio Emanuele, 0565/763-746) in the tiny town of **Castagneto Carducci** and have a pizza or *aperitivo* in the charming hamlet of **Bolgheri** itself, one hill over, with great views of the surrounding hillsides.

It is possible to visit the best wineries of Bolgheri, but you have to jump through a couple of hoops to do it. Specifically you need to arrange all visits through the **Consorzio Strada del Vino** (Costa degli Etruschi, Loc. San Guido 45, Bolgheri 57020, tel. 0565/749-768, fax 0565/749-705, www.lastradadelvino.com, sdv@infol.it). The multilingual staff will help you arrange either group or individual tours of Sassicaia, Ornellaia, Michele Satta, and other big names of the region. The tours are always guided, giving insight into the history of the wines and the techniques used to make them, and they always end with a tasting. Spring and summer are the best times to visit the area, though you can come any time of year except during the September harvest. It is best to call up to a month in advance to organize everything, though a week ahead will often suffice.

L'Andana

Tenuta La Badiola, Castiglione della Pescaia
tel. 0564/944-800, fax 0564/944-577
www.andana.it

In the first edition of this book, published in 2003, I mentioned that Bolgheri was still not quite ready for prime-time tourism, but that the region was certain to see some big changes in the near future. The next year,

Alain Ducasse chose the Maremma as the site of L'Andana, his deluxe hotel and restaurant. Housed in the former royal abode of Leopold II, the hotel combines elegantly appointed rooms, complete with stone fireplaces, and a gorgeous landscape of olive trees and grapevines. The restaurant, which seats 120, makes use of the local agriculture for its haute menu.

A Bolgheri Wine Rundown

Tenuta dell'Ornellaia's premier wine is without doubt the expensive and award-winning DOC Bolgheri Superiore, a mix of Cabernet Sauvignon and Merlot with a small amount of Cabernet Franc. The wine is aged for eighteen months in *barriques* and then in the bottle for another year. For us mortals, they make a less coddled and much more affordable red called Le Volte, as well as some very good whites. Formerly owned by an Antinori relative, Ornellaia was bought in 2002 by a consortium that includes Frescobaldi and Robert Mondavi of California.

Guado al Tasso, the jewel in the vast Antinori family crown, produces a high-end Bolgheri DOC Superiore that uses all nonnative grapes—Cabernet, Syrah, and Merlot—and is stored in new French *barriques* for a year, then racked and aged in both barrel and bottle before being released. The winery also makes a white Vermentino and a rosé called Scalabrone.

Podere Grattamacco is a highly regarded maker of a Bolgheri Rosso Superiore called Grattamacco Rosso, as well as a Bolgheri DOC white, a grappa, and an olive oil.

San Vincenzo

San Vicenzo is a popular seaside town made up of unrelentingly bland modern architecture. The one outstanding feature (other than a Michelin two-star restaurant) is a long pedestrian commercial zone that becomes site of a boisterous *passeggiata* (evening stroll) late into the night. The town is small, and if you don't keep a keen eye out, you could drive straight through it without finding the two excellent eateries here, both situated at the small port.

Tenuta San Guido, domain of the Marchese Incisa della Rochetta, makes Sassicaia, the Supertuscan that started it all. Revolutionary for an Italian wine at the time (in the 1970s), it is a fairly straightforward blend of Cabernet Sauvignon with 15 to 20 percent Cabernet Franc. It is aged in stainless steel, in *barriques*, and in the bottle before reaching the shelves. Sassicaia was the first mark to receive its own DOC designation, perhaps as acknowledgment for the trickle-down benefits it has bestowed on Italy's wine industry as a whole.

Michele Satta is best known for its fine red called Piastraia, a potent combination of Cabernet, Sangiovese, and Merlot. Satta also produces an all-Sangiovese wine called Vigna del Cavaliere, which is aged in *barriques* for a year before reaching the stores. One of the most popular wines is Diambra, a light Bolgheri Rosso that goes well with food but won't overpower subtle flavors like chicken or fish. The winery's Bolgheri Bianco is also excellent.

Enrico Santini is a small producer who came out with his first vintage in 2000 but is already putting out an excellent product. Try the strong, deep red Poggio al Moro Bolgheri Rosso DOC, or one of his white wines, and look to see much more from this winery in the future.

Gambero Rosso

Piazza della Vittoria 13, tel. 0565/701-021, fax 0565/704-542
Open Wednesday through Sunday 12:30 PM to 2 PM and 8 PM to midnight
€€€€

San Vincenzo is an unlikely and somewhat inauspicious location for a two-star restaurant, which draws little attention to itself as it overlooks a port, a turquoise sea, and a parking lot. But this tiny eatery has been plucked from obscurity and ranked with the best and brightest: it has been voted best restaurant in the country by *Gambero Rosso* magazine (no relation) in past years and been given the nod by the extremely finicky people at Michelin. Gambero Rosso is the creation of Fulvio Pierangelini, recognized as one of the top chefs on the peninsula. When *Wine Spectator* devoted a special issue to the food and wine of Tuscany, it raved, "No one in the region can cook as well as Fulvio Pierangelini, whose food exhibits vibrant clarity and intense flavor." I find Gambero Rosso a bit more formal and stuffy than the restaurants I love most, but I do agree that it serves the most thrilling fish dishes in Tuscany.

The elegant dining room is surprisingly intimate, with just seven tables oriented toward the sparkling sea. Fresh fish, large and small, along with shellfish, make up the bulk of the menu. For an antipasto, you might choose between delicate scallops cooked in lemon butter and served in their own shells, or a salad of small red mullet. Primi include a perfect risotto with thick chunks of shellfish, bright pink crayfish, and salty mussels. One of the kitchen's signature dishes is a silky chickpea soup garnished with whole prawns. Another is the fresh-made fish ravioli topped with seafood-broth cream. But if you venture away from the sea for a primo, you won't be disappointed. The chef's ravioli stuffed with pigeon and topped with a reduced cream sauce is divine. Most of the secondi focus on fresh Mediterranean fish: gilt-head bream served in a sweet reduction of wine with pear, or sea bass wrapped in pancetta. All are cooked perfectly and matched with a delicate sauce, whether sweet or savory.

Desserts might include a dark chocolate terrine, a *semifreddo* of *torrone* (almond nougat) with chocolate sauce, and an unusual assortment of *sorbetti* accompanied with little house-made cookies. The wine list deserves mention as well, not only for its excellently chosen selection of whites (important for all the fish) and reds, but also for the extremely reasonable prices. Many diners here opt for the excellent five-course tasting menu, which includes many of Pierangelini's classic dishes.

Zanzibar

Piazza del Porto 2, 0565/702-927
Open Thursday through Tuesday 8:30 AM to midnight, Wednesday 8:30 AM
to 5:30 PM
€€

Zanzibar is just a few steps down the boardwalk from Gambero Rosso, but worlds away in atmosphere. While Gambero Rosso is buttoned up, Zanzibar, with its mosaic-tile tables set outdoors next to billowing white drapery sheltering you from the sun, is where you go with sand between your toes. At once chic and minimalist in its interior design and casual in its attitude, Zanzibar is the kind of bar and fish restaurant you dream about finding at the beach: the mythical margarita in a chilled glass, the perfect plate of fried fish.

After you've had your *aperitivo*, the table is remade in preparation for dinner. The menu, handwritten on plain brown paper, is all fish (almost all of which are caught near San Vincenzo): fish soup, *fritto misto*, linguine with *frutti di mare*, and a changing selection of fish grilled over a live fire. The fish soup is heavier on the fish than on the soup, with whole prawns and other crustaceans sunbathing on the rim of a bowl holding a scant amount of delicious seafood-scented broth. The *fritto misto* (one of my favorite things to eat), served on brown paper, consists of small fish like sardines, anchovies, and red mullet.

After your meal, take a stroll through San Vincenzo's pedestrian district, where it seems as if the whole town—or possibly the whole region—is out walking, eating gelato, even shopping, since the stores here stay open until midnight.

Beaches of Southern Tuscany

If you're not too sated from the excellent food of San Vincenzo, you should visit one of this area's many fine beaches. Near Bolgheri, you'll find a plenitude of decent public beaches when you enter either at the **Marina di Donoratico** or the **Marina di Bibbona**. Take your pick between private clubs that provide *ombrelloni* and lounge chairs, and large swaths of public sand, cleaner and better cared for here than in other parts of Tuscany. If you have the time, the car, and the desire to visit the nicest beach in Tuscany, travel south past Grosseto for about an hour and a half until you reach the exit for the **Parco Naturale di Maremma**. Follow the signs first to the small town of **Alberese**, which houses the parking office for the **Marina di Alberese**. At the office you can purchase the right to park in the beach parking lot. There is a separate ticket office around the corner for visiting the park itself—what, did you think they'd make it easy for you? Rangers offer guided tours of the most interesting hikes in the park fairly early in the morning in summer, and for the rest of the day you can buy a ticket that lets you wander around specific open areas of the park. Public access is limited because of fire danger in summer, but during the rest of the year you can visit the entire park without restrictions.

To get to the beach from the parking ticket office, retrace your tracks and then turn west to the marina, where you'll encounter a barrier bar into which you insert your parking ticket and then are allowed to pass. Next, you drive on an evocative lane lined with umbrella pines to the parking lot for the Marina di Alberese, from which you can walk along several miles of uncorrupted white sandy beach. The turquoise water here is the perfect temperature for swimming amid the gentle waves.

Il Giardino dei Tarocchi

If your itinerary takes you farther south from Alberese, an artistic marvel awaits just outside the medieval hilltown of Capalbio. The iconoclastic French American artist **Niki de Saint-Phalle** is best known for her colorful, childlike, kinetic sculptures in the fountain outside the Centre Pompidou in Paris, but her true magnum opus, which took decades and dozens of assistants to create, lies in the hinterlands of southern Tuscany. The massive figures that make up her Giardino dei Tarocchi (Tarot Garden) are visible even from the Via Aurelia as you approach the site. The artist built a wonderland of giant, playful figures, some as big as buildings, covered with a sea of mosaic tiles, mirrors, and decorated ceramic. Saint-Phalle's signature "nana" figures—giant, surreal maternal personae—preside over the central fountain. Nearby you'll find an idiosyncratic chapel that looks like an igloo; a two-story piazza; and a female figure that, once entered (yes, it's all quite Freudian), becomes a psychedelic living quarters, complete with mirror-covered bedroom and bathroom, where the artist actually lived for part of the time she worked on the project. The figures, large and small, all correspond to symbols from a tarot deck but also seem to represent various aspects of humanity. The garden is a truly unique and inspiring experience, especially for kids, who are ecstatic at the opportunity to touch and crawl all over "art" without getting in trouble.

Il Giardino dei Tarocchi

Loc. Garavicchio, 0564/895-122

www.nikidesaintphalle.com

Open daily May 13 through October 20 2:30 PM to 7:30 PM and November through May on the first Sunday of each month 9 AM to 1 PM (call first to confirm)

Tickets €10.50 for adults, €6 for students and children 7 to 16, children under 7 free

When you are done here, you might also explore the nearby town of **Capalbio**, where you can walk on the walls, have an ice cream, or take in a meal at one of the multitude of attractive trattorias.

Scansano

If you'd like to continue your wine tasting in southern Tuscany, head east from Alberese to Scansano, home of the Morellino grape (a variant of Sangiovese) and birthplace of some very good red wines. The area is in the rarely visited hills to the southeast of Grosseto.

Erik Banti, a dashing figure and modern Renaissance man, has been making wine in the area since the early 1980s. In 1994, he relocated his base to Scansano (Loc. Fosso dei Molini, Scansano, tel. 0564/508-006, fax 0564/508-019, www.erikbanti.com, info@erikbanti.com; open Monday through Friday 8:30 AM to 12:30 PM and 2 PM to 6 PM, Saturday 10 AM to 1 PM and 4 PM to 7 PM). In addition to Morellino, he is harvesting relatively new acreage of Sangiovese and is also growing Merlot, Cabernet Sauvignon, Syrah, and Primitivo on recently acquired land. Unlike many wineries of the region, Banti welcomes visits and offers free wine tastings (*accidenti!*). Tastings are open to the public during normal operating hours (April through October). The estate's wine shop, which he describes as California style, also sells *salumi* and cheeses, and is open on weekends. Already recognized as a pioneer for the Morellino grape, Banti is now clearly at the forefront of accessible wine tourism in southern Tuscany.

GLOSSARY

A

Acciuga (also *alice*) = Anchovy
Aceto = Vinegar
Aceto balsamico = Balsamic vinegar
Acido = Sour, acidic
Acqua = Water
Acqua frizzante (also *acqua gassata*) =
    Sparkling water
Acqua naturale = Still water
Affogato = Gelato doused with espresso
Affumicato/a = Smoked
Aglio = Garlic
Agnello = Lamb
Albicocca = Apricot
Albume = Egg white
Alimentari = Small food shop
Alloro = Bay leaf
Al vapore = Steamed
Amaro = Bitter
Ananas = Pineapple
Anatra (also *anitra*) = Duck
Antipasto = Appetizer
Aperitivo = Before-dinner drink
Arachide = Peanut
Aragosta = Lobster
Arancia = Orange
Aringa = Herring
Arista = Roast pork
Arrosto = Roasted
Asparagi = Asparagus
Astice = Rock lobster

B

Babà = Little cake soaked in rum
Baccalà = Salt cod
Basilico = Basil

Barbabietola = Beet
Bavarese = Puddinglike dessert
Bevande = Beverages
Bicchiere = A glass
Bietola = Swiss chard
Bignè = Éclair
Birra = Beer
Biscotti = Cookies
Bistecca = Steak
Bocconcini = Little bites
Bollito = Boiled; often a shorthand for
    boiled meat
Bombolone = Doughnut
Bottarga = Dried mullet or tuna roe
Bottiglia = Bottle
Braciola = Chop (e.g., pork chop)
Branzino (also *spigola*) = Sea bass
Bresaola = Air-cured salted beef
Brioche = Croissant (in other parts of
    Italy it is often called *cornetto*)
Brodo = Broth
Bruciato = Burned
Bruschetta = Grilled bread slice rubbed
    with garlic and drizzled with olive oil
Buccia = Peel, rind (e.g., of an orange)
Budino = Pudding
Burrata = A fresh cow's milk cheese from
    the Campania region in southern
    Italy; similar to mozzarella but
    creamier
Burro = Butter

C

Caccia = Wild game
Cacciucco = Fish stew, specialty of
    Livorno

Cachi = Persimmons
Caffè = Coffee
Caffeina = Caffeine
Caffettiera = Coffeemaker
Caldo = Hot
Cameriere = Waiter
Candito = Candied
Cantucci[ni] = Biscotti
Capperi = Capers
Caprino = Goat cheese
Caraffa = Carafe
Carciofi = Artichokes
Carne = Meat
Carota = Carrot
Carpaccio = Anything served raw and thinly sliced; usually a meat or fish
Carta = Menu
Carta dei vini = Wine list
Cassa = Cash register
Castagna = Chestnut
Cavallo = Horse, horsemeat
Cavatappo = Bottle corkscrew
Cavolfiore = Cauliflower
Cavolo = Cabbage
Cavolo nero = Tuscan black cabbage
Ceci = Chickpeas
Cena = Dinner
Cenare = To dine
Cervelli = Brains
Cetriolo = Cucumber
Ciabatta = Slipper-shaped bread
Ciliegia = Cherry
Cime di rapa = Turnip leaf (bitter green)
Cinghiale = Wild boar
Cioccolata calda = Hot chocolate
Cioccolato = Chocolate
Ciotola (also *scodella*) = Bowl
Cipolla = Onion
Cocco = Coconut
Cocomero = Watermelon
Coda di rospo = Monkfish
Colazione = Breakfast

Coltello = Knife
Condividere (also *fare in due*) = To share
Coniglio = Rabbit
Conto = The bill
Contorno = Side dish
Coperto = Cover charge
Cotta/o = Cooked
Cozze = Mussels
Crema = Cream or custard
Crema chantilly = Whipped cream
Crespelle = Crepes
Crosta = Crust
Crostata = A tart, usually filled with jam
Crostini = Little toasts, usually covered with liver pâté
Crostoni = Open-faced sandwiches
Crudo = Raw
Cucchiaiata or Cucchiaio = Spoon[ful]
Cucchiaino = Little spoonful; teaspoon
Cucina = Kitchen (also used for cuisine)
Cucinare = To cook

D
Datteri = Dates
Decaffeinato = Decaffeinated coffee
Degustazione = Tasting menu
Disossato = Boned
Dolce = Sweet
Dolci = Sweets, desserts

E
Enofilo = Oenophile
Enoteca = Wine shop, wine bar
Erbe = Herbs
Etto = 100 grams (about 1/4 pound)
Extravergine = Extra virgin (olive oil)

F
Fagioli = Beans (usually "white beans" in Tuscany)
Fagiolini = Green beans

Faraona = Guinea hen

Fare la scarpetta = To soak up sauce with bread

Farro = Ancient wheat variety, sometimes translated as emmer

Fave = Fava beans

Fegatini = Chicken or rabbit liver

Fegato = Liver

Fettina = Thin slice

Fettunta = Tuscan word for bruschetta

Fichi = Figs

Fichi di India = Prickly pears

Filetto = Fillet (usually beef or fish)

Finocchio = Fennel bulb

Finocchiona = Tuscan salami made with pork and spiced with fennel

Fior di latte (sometimes *fiordilatte*) = Fresh cow's milk mozzarella

Fiori di zucca = Zucchini flowers

Fondente = Melted chocolate

Forchetta = Fork

Formaggio = Cheese

Forno = Oven; also bread bakery

Fragola = Strawberry

Freddo = Cold

Fresco = Fresh; also cool or cold

Frigorifero (also *frigo*) = Refrigerator

Frittelle = Sweet fritters

Fritto = Fried

Frutta = Fruit

Funghi = Mushrooms

Fuso = Melted

G

Gamberetto = Baby shrimp

Gambero = Shrimp

Gamberone = Big shrimp

Gelato = Ice cream

Ghiaccio = Ice

Gnocchetti = Little gnocchi

Gnocchi = Dumplings made from potato or semolina

Golosa/o = A glutton

Gorgonzola = Italian blue cheese, from Lombardy

Grana = Aged cow's milk cheese from the north, similar to Parmesan

Granchio = Crab

Granita = Crushed-ice sorbet

Grappa = Hard alcohol made from grape pomace

Grasso = Fat

Grigliata = Grilled

Guanciale = Pork cheek meat

Guscio = Peel or shell (e.g., of a nut, egg, fava bean)

I

Insalata = Salad

Insalatone = Big salad

Integrale = Whole wheat

In umido = Braised in sauce

Involtino = Anything rolled in a cylindrical shape

Inzimino = A dish of squid (usually) cooked in spicy tomato sauce

L

Lampone = Raspberry

Lampredotto = Offal from the fourth cow stomach

Lardo di Colonnata = Cured pork fat from Colonnata

Latte = Milk

Lattina = Can

Lattuga = Lettuce

Lenticchie = Lentils

Lepre = Hare

Lesso = Boiled

Lievito di birra = Yeast

Limoncello = Lemon liqueur

Limone = Lemon

Litro = Liter

Lombatina di vitella = Veal chop

M

Macedonia = Fruit salad
Macinato = Ground
Maiale = Pork
Mais = Corn
Mancia = A tip
Mandorla = Almond
Manzo = Beef
Marmellata = Fruit jam
Marzapane = Marzipan
Mascarpone = Fresh cow's milk cheese, from Lombardy
Mela = Apple
Melanzana = Eggplant
Melone = Melon
Menta = Mint
Mezzo kilo = Half a kilo (about 1 pound)
Mezzo litro = Half liter
Mezzo stagionato = Semi aged (cheese)
Miele = Honey
Minestra = A broth with vegetables and sometimes rice or pasta
Mirtillo = Blueberry
Misto = Mixed
Mora = Blackberry
Mortadella = Bologna
Mostarda (also *senape*) = Usually refers to tangy chutney made with fruit and mustard seed, typical of Modena
Mozzarella di bufala = Prized mozzarella made from buffalo's milk

N, O

Nespola = Loquat, medlar
Nocciola = Hazelnut
Noce = Nut (usually walnut)
Nostrale = Locally grown or raised
Oca = Goose

Olio = Oil
Olio di oliva/uliva = Olive oil
Olio di semi = Sunflower seed oil
Orata = Gilt-head bream
Osso = Bone
Ostrica = Oyster

P

Padella = Pan
Pancetta = Salt-cured bacon
Pane = Bread
Panino = Sandwich (or sandwich roll)
Panna = Cream
Panna cotta = Dessert made of cooked cream
Panzanella = Florentine summer bread salad
Pappa al pomodoro = Florentine tomato-bread soup
Pappardelle = Long, wide fresh pasta
Parmigiano = Parmesan cheese
Passato = Thick puréed bean and/or vegetable soup
Pasta = Pasta as used in English; dough; a pastry such as brioche
Pasto = A meal
Patata = Potato
Pecorino Toscano = Tuscan cheese made from sheep's milk
Pentola = Pot
Pepe = Pepper
Peperoncino = Dried hot red pepper
Peperone = Pepper (bell, red, etc.)
Peposo/a = Tuscan beef stew with whole peppercorns
Pera = Pear
Pesce = Fish
Pesce spada = Swordfish
Petto = Breast
Piatto = Plate
Piccante = Spicy
Piccione = Pigeon

Pici = Thick rustic handmade spaghetti

Pinoli = Pine nuts

Pinzimonio = Raw vegetables with salt and oil for dipping

Piselli = Peas

Pizzico = A pinch (e.g., of salt)

Pollo = Chicken

Polpetta = Meatball

Polpo = Octopus

Pomodorini = Cherry tomatoes

Pomodoro = Tomato

Pompelmo = Grapefruit

Porchetta = Pork stuffed with herbs and cooked slowly on a spit

Porcini = Aromatic mushrooms available fresh in the fall and dried year-round

Porro = Leek

Pranzare = To have lunch

Pranzo = Lunch

Prezzemolo = Parsley

Prosciutto = General term for ham

Prosciutto cotto = Cooked ham

Prosciutto crudo = Raw cured ham

Prugna = Prune

Purè = Mashed potatoes

Q, R

Quaglia = Quail

Ragù = Meat sauce for pasta

Ribollita = Tuscan bread-bean-kale soup

Ricetta = Recipe

Ricevuta (also *scontrino*) = Receipt

Ricotta = Light, fresh cheese made from either cow's or sheep's milk

Ripieno = Stuffed

Riso = Rice

Risotto = Slow-boiled rice dish

Rombo = Turbot

Rosmarino (also *ramerino*) = Rosemary

Rucola (also *ruchetta*) = Arugula

S

Salame = Salami

Sale = Salt

Salmone = Salmon

Salsa = Sauce

Salsiccia = Sausage

Saltato = Sautéed quickly in oil

Salumi = General term for cured meats

Salvia = Sage

Sarde = Sardines

Scalogno = Shallot

Scampi = Crayfish

Scamorza = Cow's milk cheese that comes shaped like a pear with golden rind

Scarola = Escarole

Schiacciata = Tuscan version of focaccia

Scodella (also *ciotola*) = Bowl

Scontrino (also *ricevuta*) = Receipt

Sedano = Celery

Semifreddo = Sweet frozen mousse

Senape = Mustard

Seppia = Squid

Sfogliatelle = A flaky, ricotta-stuffed pastry

Soffritto = Mix of carrot, celery, and onion used as a base for most stocks and sauces

Soppressata = Headcheese

Speck = Smoked pork, typical of Alto Adige

Spezzatino = Beef stew

Spiedini = Skewered

Spigola (also *branzino*) = Sea bass

Spinaci = Spinach

Spumante = Italian sparkling white wine

Spuntino = Snack

Stagionato = Aged (as for cheese)

Stracchino = Very creamy, tangy cow's milk cheese from northern Italy

Stracotto = Beef braised in wine
Strutto = Lard (uncured)
Sugo = Meat sauce
Surgelato = Frozen
Susina = Plum

T

Tacchino = Turkey
Tagliata = Sliced, usually a plate of sliced steak
Taleggio = Pungent, tangy cow's milk cheese, from Lombardy
Tartufo bianco = White truffle
Tartufo nero = Black truffle
Tè = Tea
Tè deteinato = Decaffeinated tea
Tiepido = Warm
Timo = Thyme
Tomino = Small round of goat or other soft cheese, often baked
Tonno = Tuna
Torta = Cake, pie, tart
Torta della nonna = Florentine custard tart
Tovaglia = Tablecloth
Tovagliolo = Napkin
Triglia = Red mullet
Trippa = Tripe
Trota = Trout

U

Uovo = Egg
Uovo sodo = Hard-boiled egg

Uva = Grape
Uva passa = Raisins (also *uvetta* and *sultana*)

V

Vaniglia = Vanilla
Verdure = Vegetables
Verza = Dark, leafy round cabbage
Vino = Wine
Vino della casa = House wine
Vino novello = New wine, no aging
Vin santo = Sweet dessert wine, from Tuscany
Vino sfuso = Wine from a vat
Vitello = Veal
Vitellone = Veal from calf slaughtered between twelve and eighteen months
Vongole = Clams

Z

Zabaglione = Custard made with egg, cream, and Marsala wine
Zafferano = Saffron
Zampone = Pig's trotter
Zenzero = Ginger
Zibibbo = Sicilian dessert wine (also name of the grape)
Zucca = Squash, pumpkin
Zucchero = Sugar
Zucchine = Zucchini
Zuccotto = Tuscan dessert of sponge cake, ricotta, and whipped cream
Zuppa = Thick soup

INDEX

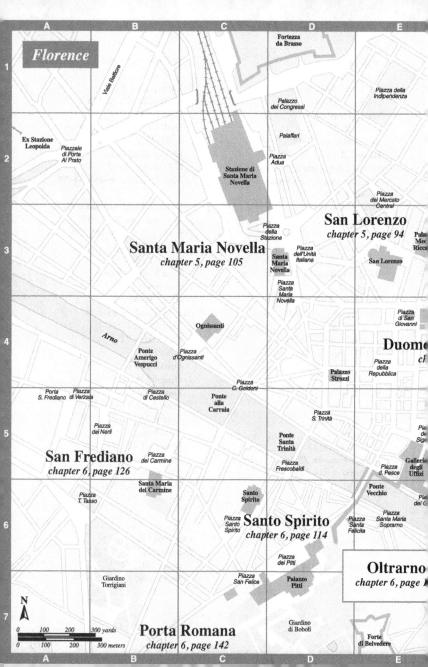

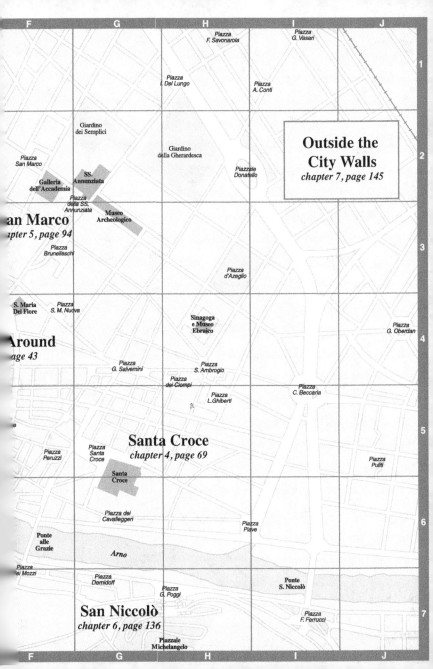

Piazza F. Savonarola

Piazza G. Vasari

Piazza I. Del Lungo

Piazza A. Conti

Giardino dei Semplici

Giardino della Gherardesca

Piazza San Marco

Outside the City Walls
chapter 7, page 145

SS. Annunziata

Galleria dell'Accademia

Piazzale Donatello

Piazza della SS. Annunziata

Museo Archeologico

San Marco
chapter 5, page 94

Piazza Brunelleschi

Piazza d'Azeglio

S. Maria Del Fiore

Piazza S. M. Nuova

Around
age 43

Sinagoga e Museo Ebraico

Piazza G. Oberdan

Piazza G. Salvemini

Piazza S. Ambrogio

Piazza dei Ciompi

Piazza L. Ghiberti

Piazza C. Beccaria

Piazza Peruzzi

Piazza Santa Croce

Santa Croce
chapter 4, page 69

Piazza Puliti

Santa Croce

Piazza dei Cavalleggeri

Piazza Piave

Ponte alle Grazie

Arno

ei Mozzi

Piazza Demidoff

Piazza G. Poggi

Ponte S. Niccolò

San Niccolò
chapter 6, page 136

Piazza F. Ferrucci

Piazzale Michelangelo

F   G   H   I   J

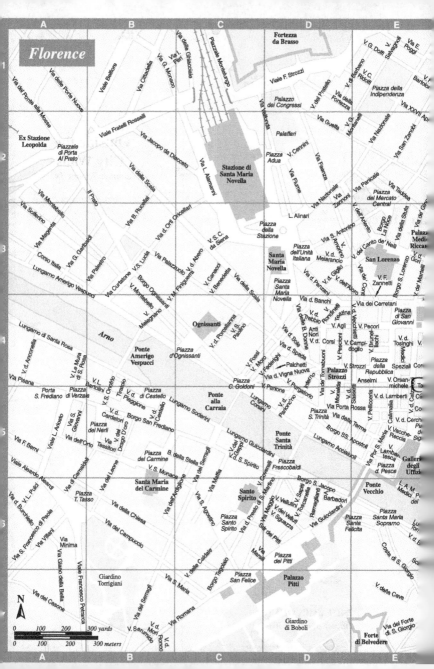

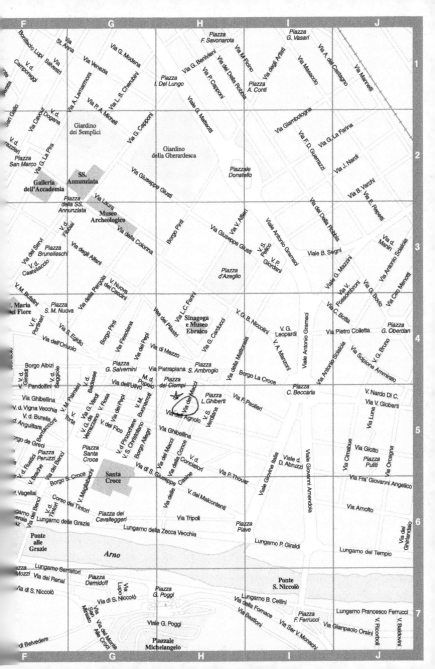

EMILY WISE MILLER is a food and travel writer based in Florence. She has written and edited travel guides to Italy, Great Britain, and the Pacific Northwest; edited a variety of cookbooks for Williams-Sonoma; and written on food, travel, and culture for the *Times* of London, the *San Francisco Chronicle*, Salon.com, and other publications.